To Archie,
Thank you
for your support.
Nada M.
11/18/06

Aflame
With The
Spirit:

Philip
the Evangelist

By

Vada M. Gipson

A sequel to The Quests

© 2006 Vada M. Gipson. All rights reserved.

No part of this book may be reproduced, stored in a retrieval system, or transmitted by any means without the written permission of the author.

First published by AuthorHouse 3/17/2006

ISBN: 1-4259-0648-6 (sc)

Library of Congress Control Number: 2005910860

Printed in the United States of America
Bloomington, Indiana

This book is printed on acid-free paper.

1663 LIBERTY DRIVE, SUITE 200
BLOOMINGTON, INDIANA 47403
(800) 839-8640
WWW.AUTHORHOUSE.COM

Chapter One

"Judas Iscariot, your partner is-- "A name was drawn from the basket. "--Philip Bar Joseph of Bethsaida."

Oh no! Why was my name drawn to travel with him? His idea that Jesus will be a military leader doesn't coincide with mine.

Philip looked around for Judas. All seventy disciples and camp followers were sitting on the ground or rock outcroppings. He was a distance away and looking at Philip. Judas nodded and Philip returned his acknowledgment.

Thirty-five pairs were being matched at this drawing. The twelve of Jesus' inner circle were going out with twelve from the outer circle, plus forty-six others.

Matthew, a former tax collector--one of the original followers, was in charge of the drawing. When all names were drawn, he said, "The Master wants to know if any of you have a preference as to where you will be sent?"

Several of the apostles requested to return to villages where they had been on the first trip. The others were willing to accept whatever destination came out of the basket. Matthew started drawing names of places, and the pairs took them in the order their own names were drawn: Dan/Caesarea Philippi, Tyre, Sidon, Damascus, Joppa, Beersheba, and on he went. Philip experienced a thrill of excitement as his and Judas' turn was near-- *where would they be sent?*

"Dor by the Sea," Matthew called out. Philip exchanged looks with Judas. He couldn't tell by his reaction how Judas felt. It excited Philip.

They were encamped in Jesus' favorite retreat in the mountains west of Capernaum. Philip had never been any farther west, and he was happy for the chance to go to the great sea.

Matthew kept on calling names of towns and villages until thirty-five had been drawn.

Jesus said, "You are to take nothing with you, no coins, no food, no extra clothing. You are to talk to no one you meet on the road."

Philip, who was seated near the front of the group, glanced around and could see how intensely everyone was listening. All eyes were on the Master.

"You may accept hospitality of householders along the way to your destination."

Someone asked, "How will we know that we are welcome?"

Jesus answered, "This is how: When your knock is answered, pass the peace, your 'Shalom.' If you are invited in, stay there. If not, leave the place and go on your way."

"What do we do when we reach our village?"

"The same thing, except that you shall stay in one place all the time you are there. If you can find no one to give you food and shelter, shake the dust of the village from your sandals and leave."

"Tell us what we are to do while we are there."

Impatiently he responded, "How long have you been with me? And you need to have me tell you every move?" Jesus then explained, "You are to preach 'The kingdom of God is near,' and you are to heal the sick and infirm

Vada M Gipson

and teach what you have learned from me. Are there any other questions?"

No one ventured to ask. Jesus said, "Some of you have long distances to travel. I want you to have time to start a fellowship of disciples, so allow forty days for the round trip. If your village will not accept you, and neither will the next, move on and help your brothers in their village. I'll be waiting for you here. Go now. Take my love and the love of my Father, who sent me, with you. You will be kept safe. Shalom."

"Shalom," was returned by all seventy men.

Philip had become a disciple of Jesus' within a week of his healing. He had returned home and celebrated with family and friends his freedom from paralysis. He walked all over the village of Bethsaida, which had been renamed "Julias" after Caesar's wife, too happy to feel any animosity. Instead, he felt gratitude for the tenacity of his brothers that led him to being lowered through the roof of that house in Capernaum.

As his strength returned, he started going to the encampment to be with the Master. After about six weeks, he was chosen to be

Aflame With The Spirit: Philip the Evangelist

in the second group to be sent out. He was thrilled.

Thereafter followed a period of about six weeks of intense training. He lived at the camp. During this time the newer disciples were taught how to heal. They also were given special classes in how the Law was being confirmed and strengthened. Special emphasis was made on God's love for humankind. Philip felt awed at being given this responsibility.

Before departing on this big adventure, he asked his mother-in-law, Zipporah, "Would it be too much for you to take all four of my girls to live with you?" The dying request of his wife, Hannah, was that her parents raise their four daughters.

She responded, "Philip, I was going to ask for Esther again, but if I could have the others, too, I would be very happy." Zipporah had kept the last baby for a year, and thereafter held a class at Philip's parents home where other three girls lived, teaching them reading and writing.

"Thank you, Mother. I think it's important for them to be together. They are doing so well under your tutoring, you can continue their lessons while they're being trained to be wives and mothers."

"It will be my pleasure."

So, amid tears and laughter, the four sisters took their belongings from Philip's father's home to that of Zipporah and her second husband, Ishi.

Chapter Two

"Have you been to Dor?" Philip asked Judas as they left the camp and headed south on the road along the shore of the Sea of Galilee. Other pairs were traveling the same road.

"Yes."

"Then you know how to get there?"

"We must go to Nazareth. The shortest route from there is through Samaria to Caesarea."

"Caesarea? How long do you think it will take us?"

"We'll go to Magdala for tonight. We should get to Nazareth tomorrow night. Two or three more days should do it."

After walking a few paces in silence, Philip asked, "What's it like, Dor?"

"It's an old Canaanite fishing village. They're called Phoenicians now."

Philip thought on that information for a short distance, then asked, "Are many Jews there?"

Judas replied emphatically, "No, there are not. I'm surprised it was on the list of places to go."

Philip hesitantly asked, "Our work is to be with the Jews, isn't it?"

"Yes!" He answered impatiently. "'The lost tribes of Israel' is what he told us before."

Philip was fearful he was treading on some kind of inner feeling of Judas, and kept his silence.

Judas was about thirty, the same age as Philip. He was not as tall as Philip; he had black hair, beard, and dark eyes. Philip had dark hair and beard with fair skin and blue eyes. Judas moved quickly with no wasted motion, as if he were impatient to get on with life.

After about ten minutes Philip asked, "Are you from Galilee?"

"No. My father's home is in Judea, a small town called Kerioth in the Negev."

"That's a long way from here, isn't it?"

"Yes."

Aflame With The Spirit: Philip the Evangelist

"The Master must have great trust in you since he has chosen you to take care of the money for the group. How did you find him?"

Judas unexpectedly laughed, "I think he found me, rather than I finding him."

"What do you mean?"

After giving some thought to his answer, Judas said, "I was looking for a group up here that I'd heard about. It had been started by a Judas of Galilee about twenty-five years ago."

Philip, trying to remember the event, asked, "Was that the Judas, who was killed when he led a revolt against Rome at the time of the census?"

"The same. His belief, and it's my belief, was that our only ruler and Lord is God."

"Did you find the sect?"

"No. I have since learned of individuals who have knowledge of it, but I'm satisfied now in following Jesus."

"You said he found you. How did that happen?"

"I was at the Jordan listening to John the baptizer when he was arrested by Herod's soldiers--"

Philip stopped walking and almost shouted, "I was there, too! I saw it from across the river."

Judas stopped too, and looking at him asked, "Did you have the same lost feeling that I had?"

"Indeed I did!" As they resumed their walking, Philip said, "Go ahead with your story."

"Well, I went up the road toward Galilee, and found another group baptizing, just like John was. So I stayed to listen."

"Who was it?"

"Jesus' disciples John and James. Peter and Andrew were there, too. Of course, I didn't know any of them yet. Jesus was in the crowd, healing and teaching."

"That must have been a thrill."

"Yes, it was--because he knew my name! He came to where I was standing and said, 'Judas, you are searching for a leader. Try me.'"

When Judas hesitated, Philip exclaimed, "What an invitation! What did you say?"

"Well, I didn't know if I wanted to try following him or not. I didn't know him or anything about him. But something about his eyes, and he knew my name--and my quest--and I had witnessed his healing people and the feeling he had for them."

"So?"

Aflame With The Spirit: Philip the Evangelist

"I said, 'Rabbi, I will give it a try.' And I've been following him ever since. We're coming to Magdala."

"Do you know anyone here?"

"Yes. Mary is a camp follower. She has invited all of us to stay at her place tonight."

Philip remembered hearing about the healing of Mary Magdalene, and had seen her in camp. He felt grateful for her hospitality and generosity.

After a good meal and a night's rest at the home of Mary, Philip, Judas and three other pairs took the road going southwest out of Magdala. It took them through the mountains to Nazareth.

They knew Jesus' family was at Nazareth. While the townspeople were opposed to Jesus' teachings, and his brothers were not followers, his mother would be hospitable. So the second night out was spent in the home of Mary, mother of Jesus.

After they had lain down for the night, Judas said to Philip, "Are you willing to go through Samaria tomorrow?"

"Why do you ask?"

"On the other mission, we were told specifically to stay out of Samaria."

"What other option do we have?"

"We can go north from here to Cana, and come out at Ptolemais on the great sea. We will be north of Mount Carmel, and will have to go around the toe of it to get to Dor. It will take at least a day longer that way."

Philip hesitated. He knew that at the time of the exile to Babylon, hundreds of years before, many Hebrews who were left behind intermarried with natives in Samaria. Some also accepted other gods. Therefore, pureblood Jews refrained from any contact with the people. Finally he asked, "If we go through Samaria, how much contact will we have with the people?"

"We shouldn't have any until we get to Caesarea."

Dawn the next morning, after morning prayers, found them on the road going south out of Nazareth. They were alone as the others took the road north out of town. After leaving the Plain of Esdraelon, the road followed canyons and gaps in the Carmel Mountains.

Philip said, "These ravines are dangerous to go through alone, aren't they?"

"What do you mean, 'dangerous'?"

Aflame With The Spirit: Philip the Evangelist

"Bandits hide in this country, don't they?"

"They are no concern to us. They can see that we carry nothing to rob us of, and besides they are just like us, homeless and hungry."

"You sound like you're acquainted with them."

Judas hesitated before saying, "I am. I have had to resort to their way of life at times. When you have lost everything you own, what else can you do?"

Philip pondered this statement for a few steps. Finally he said, "I guess I've lived a sheltered life. My sect did not get involved in politics. That way Herod left us alone. We gave our tithes to God, and offerings on festival days, but we were not required to pay the government any taxes. That was the trade-off."

"Well, let me tell you a few things. Landowners and peasants not only gladly gave their tithe and offerings to their priests, and taxes for the temple, but were taxed an additional amount, up to thirty percent, by governmental rulers, and sometimes were asked to come up with more."

"Thirty percent! That would take half or more of their crops, just to pay the tithes and taxes and keep enough seed for the next year."

"Then a famine comes along. When crops fail, the revenue goes down, so the taxes are raised to support the high-living rulers, their armies, buildings and conquests."

"What happens when a farmer can't pay his taxes?"

Judas momentarily stopped in his tracks and quickly asked in a loud voice, "What do you think? He loses his land!" He started walking again, "He goes in search of work to support himself and his family. Sometimes he has to resort to banditry."

"No wonder there are revolts now and then against the rulers."

"The whole country is looking for a messiah to organize the common people and fight off the yoke of foreign domination. I think Jesus is the man. With his ability to perform miracles, he can call on angels to come and help."

Philip hesitated before responding. "What kinds of miracles have you seen him do?"

"Well, he healed you of your paralysis. Wasn't that a miracle?"

"Yes, indeed, but he has been healing all kinds of sickness. Have you seen him call on angels?"

Aflame With The Spirit: Philip the Evangelist

"No, but I saw him change water into wine at a wedding in Cana. And he fed thousands of people at his camp in the mountains with just a few loaves of bread and fish."

"Jesus doesn't strike me as a leader who would call on angels to help wipe out people. He teaches that each person is precious to God, even though he is our enemy, we should love them."

"I know that's what he's teaching now. But I think he is just doing that to get a big following without alerting Herod or Pilate to the possibility of an insurrection. He'd be killed in an instant if they thought he was organizing an army."

Philip had no response. Judas continued, "We are on a recruitment drive, you and me and the other sixty-eight. He told us to preach 'The kingdom of God is at hand.' Doesn't that sound like a password to the common people that he is willing to lead them in a fight to free our land of foreign rulers?"

After some moment's thought, Philip said, "No. He teaches with parables, with that I will agree. But organizing an army, no. I wouldn't be here, if I thought that was the reason."

"Stick around for a year. Give him time. You'll see."

"If I detect that kind of movement, I'll withdraw. I believe as much as you do that God only is our ruler. And it would be more peaceful to have the foreign powers out of our land. But, regardless of who is in the government, God still rules my heart and life. I shall not be involved in an uprising."

"You will be leaving us, then."

Philip replied, "Time will tell."

The two fell silent and walked along, each thinking divergent thoughts.

Chapter Three

After the sun had set, before dusk had turned to night, they came to a house near the road.

Judas said, "Let's see if we can find lodging here for the night."

Their arrival was announced by barking dogs long before they came to the house. The need to knock was removed by the householder standing in the door of the courtyard quieting his animals.

Judas said, "Shalom. We come in peace. May we lodge with you for the night?"

"Aren't you Jews? Can you pay?"

"Yes, we are Jews and no, we can't pay. We have no money, nor food."

"Go on your way. I can't afford to take in all you beggars who come along this road. Especially Jews!"

Philip asked, "Sir, please tell us--is there a safe resting place nearby where we could wash and maybe find some berries?"

After hesitating for a moment, scrutinizing them closely, he said, "Oh, all right, you can sleep in the courtyard."

They both answered, "Thank you."

"Out in back is a stream where you can wash. The vines out there have been picked once, but you'll find plenty of berries."

"That will be wonderful. Thank you again," Philip responded.

Judas and Philip followed the path to the creek. Taking off their robes, they left them on a rock and went into the pool of water that had been made in the bed of the shallow stream. "This feels good," Philip remarked.

A twig snapped. They stood perfectly still and listened.

After a few seconds of silence they relaxed. Judas said, "A cool dip after a long walk--" The soft sound of footsteps interrupted his thought.

"Who is there?" Judas called.

Philip felt very vulnerable--no clothes or weapon.

"Show yourself. We know you're hiding in the brush," Judas commanded.

Five figures emerged and walked slowly toward where Philip and Judas had laid their robes.

"You'll find nothing. We're traveling light," Judas said.

"We'll just take a look for ourselves," one of the men replied as he picked up one robe and then the other, feeling for pouches. Finding nothing he threw them back down.

"You're as bad off as we are. We may as well bathe together." With that he started to disrobe. The other men followed his actions, and soon the pool had seven men in it.

The leader said to Judas, "You look familiar. Do I know you?"

Judas studied his features, "You may. Are you Shemer of Samaria City?"

The man laughed, "I am! And who are you?"

"Judas of Kerioth. I think we may have done some banditry together."

Philip was beginning to breath easier. He decided Judas was a good partner to be with after all.

Shemer laughed. "What are you doing in this territory?"

"Just passing through. My partner and I are followers of Jesus of Nazareth, and are on a mission for him to Dor in Phoenicia."

"When you said you are traveling light, you weren't making it up. How can you be on a mission and not have a few shekels on you?" Shemer asked.

"Our master forbade us to bring anything." With a chuckle, Judas added, "He knew scoundrels like you would rob us."

"Your Jesus sounds like a very wise man."

"He is. You'll hear a lot more about him as time goes by. Be ready to put in with him when you have the chance."

Shemer said, "All right. I'll remember his name. Now I think I'll get dressed and see if there are any berries left on the bushes."

Judas said, "We'll join you, if you don't mind. We're hungry, too."

So Philip found himself picking berries alongside a brigand of robbers, and enjoying the protection they were giving him. They ate their fill that night and again the next morning before departing for Caesarea, having slept in the courtyard.

Chapter Four

"Is that the great sea?" Philip said while staring ahead. He and Judas had started the long descent to the plains below, Philip stopping and putting out his arm to halt Judas.

"That's it. We'll be able to see it better when we get a little farther along. Big isn't it?"

"I can't see the far shore. And so blue! What a sight!"

The ravine widened and sloped down onto level ground, suitable for farming. Philip and Judas found plenty of food along the path to sustain their energy. At last Caesarea came into view. It was late afternoon by the time they entered the east gate of the walled city.

Philip said, "This is a very big town. Can you tell me about it?"

Judas answered, "It was built by old Herod, to make a seaport for this part of the world." He hesitated, continuing, "He built a stadium and gymnasium--copying the Greeks." His voice rising in indignation he added, "His palace is supposed to be fit for a Roman king."

Philip thought on that information for a short distance. He asked, "Since it is at the sea, are there many Jews here?"

Judas replied emphatically, "No, there are not. There aren't many Samaritans, either, even though it's in their country. Greeks and Romans outnumber both the Jews and Samaritans by quite a lot. Citizens of all countries of the world are coming and going."

I wonder where we will sleep tonight? Aloud Philip said "I think we would present ourselves in a better light to a prospective householder if we were to bathe and clean ourselves. Do you know if there are public baths here?"

Judas paused before answering, "Yes, if I remember correctly, there are some Roman-style baths, but we'll have to ask where they are. And they may not be free."

As they walked along the street, they studied each residence, looking for a sign or symbol of Jewry. They reached the edge of the Forum, a huge area with monumental buildings. It was built at the main intersection of the east-west road with the north-south

Aflame With The Spirit: Philip the Evangelist

highway. Judas asked a passer-by in the Aramaic language, "Are there public baths in the Forum?"

He replied in Greek, "I don't understand you."

Judas then asked the question in Hebrew.

Again the passer-by said he did not understand.

Philip, sizing-up the situation, asked the question in Greek.

The man smiled and said, "Yes," and gave Philip directions.

They started on their way. Judas said, "I knew the city was occupied by foreigners, but I didn't expect not to be understood when I spoke the native tongue."

Philip replied, "Surely we'll find our people somewhere in this place. I'm not too fluent in Greek, either."

At the baths, they were ushered to the one for men. They disrobed and stepped into the water. An attendant came to take their robes to be shaken and brushed. Judas spoke up, "We have no money to pay for your services-- sir."

A bright beaming smile wreathed the face of the young man. He said, "You speak

Vada M Gipson

Aramaic! It's so good to hear my own language."

"Praise the Lord," Philip said, "We've found some of our people!"

The lad continued, "I'll be glad to do your robes for free. Where are you staying?"

Judas answered, "We haven't found a host yet. We are on our way to Dor. Do you know where we can go for the night?"

"You can come home with me. My father will be pleased."

Overjoyed, Philip said, "Thank you, very much."

Thus Judas and Philip were introduced to Abraham of Caesarea, who welcomed them into his home as though they were his own sons.

Chapter Five

"We appreciate your hospitality," Philip said to Abraham after he and Judas had shared the evening meal with him and his son Elmadam. They were seated at the twelve-inch high dining table in the courtyard. Philip and Elmadam were on one side, Abraham and Judas on the other.

"It's my pleasure to have you here. We don't have many Hebrews come to Caesarea. What do you do for a living?"

"I'm a scrivener, sir. If I were to be here longer than just overnight, I'd be happy to help you with your correspondence."

"Well, thank you, Philip. I wish you could stay for a while. I do have some letters that need to be written. I can write, but it's a chore."

Judas said, "I'm a farmer. Before we leave tomorrow I can help you with your garden work."

Abraham, turning to look at Judas, replied, "Now that offer is very timely. My wife hasn't been feeling well, and had to hire people to help with the house and garden work."

Philip said, "Perhaps we can serve her in a more important way."

Abraham, turning to Philip, asked, "How's that?"

Philip looked at Judas. Judas nodded for him to answer the question.

"Judas and I have been taught by our rabbi how to heal."

Abraham perceptibly pulled back. "How to heal?"

"Yes, Jesus, our master, can heal any infirmity. He receives his power from God. He calls God his father."

At this affront to Abraham's faith, he drew back. He looked at Judas, at Elmadam, and back at Philip.

Philip continued, pretending not to notice Abraham taking exception to God being called Jesus' father. "If you and your wife would care to have us--"

"Elmadam, go fetch your mother," commanded Abraham, interrupting Philip.

"She's on the pallet in her room, Father. She may be too weak to come down."

Aflame With The Spirit: Philip the Evangelist

Philip said, "If you don't mind, we can go to her."

"No, I don't mind. Come! Follow me." He immediately arose and led them up the stairs to the upper chamber.

When they reached her room, Abraham knelt beside his wife's bed on the floor and said, "Our houseguests say they have been taught how to heal. Would you like for them to try to cure your ailment?"

A very weak and pale woman of about thirty-five years was startled by this intrusion into her room. She looked first at Philip and Judas, and then stared at her husband, trying to comprehend what he had said.

Philip knelt beside Abraham. "What is your name, dear woman?" Out of compassion he took her hand.

"Leah," came the weak response.

Calmly and tenderly Philip said, "Leah, I am Philip of Julias, and this is Judas of Kerioth. We are on a mission to Dor representing our rabbi, Jesus of Nazareth. We are to preach 'The kingdom of God is near,' and to teach what he has taught us. We've also been instructed to heal any one who desires it. Would you like to be made well?"

"Oh yes," she whispered as a slight smile curved her lips.

Abraham stood and moved back, and Judas took his place beside her bed. He leaned over her, placing one hand on her forehead, the other he held upward. He said in a commanding voice, "In the name of Jesus your ailments are cured!"

Judas relaxed, but Philip continued to hold her hand. All eyes in the room were on her. Within moments color returned to her cheeks. Her eyes, earlier dulled with fever, became clear and had a sparkle. She breathed deeply and softly said, "I do feel better." Inhaling again, and in a stronger voice added, "Oh, yes! I am feeling--I don't hurt anywhere. I feel--I'm well enough to get up!"

Philip said, "You rest, and take it easy to fully regain your strength. You are well, and you will be strong again."

"I feel like getting up right now," she replied as she withdrew her hand from Philip's and raised herself up on her elbows.

"Just be careful not to overdo, until you've regained your strength," Judas added as he and Philip rose to their feet.

Leah then stood on her feet.

Aflame With The Spirit: Philip the Evangelist

Abraham and Elmadam were wide-eyed, astonished. Tears started down Abraham's face, "Praise God, praise God!" he said, "She's cured! I've never seen anything like this." Then to his wife, asked, "How do you feel, Leah?"

"I feel wonderful, better than I've ever felt. I think I had more cured than my fever." Grabbing Judas' and Philip's hands, "How can I repay you?" She started to weep, sobbing, "I can't believe I am feeling so well." And again, "How can I ever repay you?"

"You already have, dear lady," said Judas. Both he and Philip were smiling.

Regaining her composure she walked to Abraham, who threw his arms around her and gently held her close, their tear-soaked faces buried in each other's robes.

Elmadam, looking on, not knowing how to react to what he was witnessing, started to cry and laugh at the same time. He turned his face upward and yelled, "Bless You dear God. Bless You and bless Judas and Philip."

Judas and Philip turned to leave the room. Abraham released Leah as he asked her, "Do you feel strong enough to come downstairs? I want to know more about this Jesus."

"Oh yes. I'm hungry. I'm going to see if there's anything left in the kitchen."

The men talked late into the night, Philip telling about Jesus' healing of his paralysis. Judas told of others who had been blind, deaf, mute, inflicted with evil spirits, and all sorts of disease.

Finally Abraham said, "We don't have a synagogue, but we have a meeting house that takes the place of one. Will you come with us tomorrow night for Sabbath Eve?"

Philip looked at Judas, who was looking at him questioningly.

Abraham continued, "I want my friends to meet you and hear what you have to say about Jesus."

Philip said to Judas, "Our mission is 'to the lost tribes of Abraham.' Perhaps we can tarry here until after the Sabbath and then go to Dor? What do you say?"

"I think the Master would approve. Let's do it."

The next day Philip and Judas both worked in Leah's garden until Abraham came home from his place of business. Leah was well and kept the hired girl busy all day helping

Aflame With The Spirit: Philip the Evangelist

to prepare for the Sabbath, and caring for the produce the men were bringing from the garden.

Abraham said to Philip, "Here are some records of shipments. Three times now, there's been a shortage. I need to let the shipper know."

"You're in the import business?"

"I also export. I rarely have a problem."

"All right. Tell me what you want written."

"Just tell him, in a nice way, about the shortage and that he won't get credit for the merchandise until I receive it. That is, when we settle our accounts, I want us to agree."

Abraham supplied Philip with a writing reed, ink and a scroll, and Philip set about composing the letter.

He finished just before the sun set, the beginning of Sabbath. The family and Philip and Judas went to the meetinghouse. Philip was curious what a "meetinghouse" would be like. He found it was constructed much like a residence, but larger, and had no library for teaching, as the synagogues do.

Leah's friends were surprised to see her looking so healthy. The women continued chattering in their segregated area until Abraham moved to the dais in the front to introduce his houseguests. Philip noticed that, as in synagogues, the able-bodied men and women stood. Girls and small children were kept with their mothers. Boys from the age of five were allowed to be with the men. He estimated fifty adults were in attendance.

"Friends, my home has been honored with the presence of two men who are followers of a man named Jesus from Nazareth. They are on their way to Dor to tell our people there something we all have been waiting to hear since the time of David: the kingdom of God is near."

Philip was aware of a rustle from the congregation indicating a movement of bodies. Breaths were inhaled loudly enough for him to hear.

"To show the source of authority of that statement, their leader, Jesus, has taught them how to heal. Did you see Leah, my wife? Doesn't she look well?"

Several men turned to pick Leah out of the group of women.

Abraham continued, "These men are responsible for her being in good health today. They gave her life when she appeared to be dying. I can't thank God enough for that. I

Aflame With The Spirit: Philip the Evangelist

want to hear more about this man, don't you? Philip, will you talk first?"

Philip looked at Judas, who nodded for him to accept the invitation. Philip said, "I see you have the Isaiah scroll. May I read from it?"

Elmadam quickly brought the scroll to Philip, who turned to the passage he was looking for. He read, "A voice cries, 'In the wilderness prepare the way of the Lord, make straight in the desert a roadway for our God.'"

Philip then sat on a stool with long legs, following the custom in his synagogue of the rabbi standing to read the scriptures and sitting to teach.

"Have you heard of John the Baptist?"

"No" came from some of the listeners. A few said, "Yes."

"What we have to tell you really starts with John. Judas and I were both privileged to have seen John. He is dead now--beheaded by Herod."

Gasps and low comments were heard.

"We have accepted John as the fulfillment of Isaiah's prophecy. He was the forerunner preparing the way for our leader, Jesus."

Philip told about John's ministry and message. Then, standing, he said, "My companion, Judas, can tell you about Jesus.

He's been a follower longer than me." And he stepped off the dais to stand by Abraham.

Judas went to the Isaiah scroll, found the scripture and read, "The Spirit of the Lord is on me because he has blessed me to preach good news to the needy. He has sent me to give release to the captives, and sight to the blind; to free the oppressed, and to proclaim the acceptable year of the Lord."

He then sat down, and said, "I was with Jesus of Nazareth in his home synagogue when he read this same prophecy, and after he sat down said, 'Today this scripture has been fulfilled in your hearing.'"

Gasps and audible commentary rumbled through the room.

"I have been a witness to his healings, teaching and preaching, and I am satisfied that he has fulfilled the prophecy, even curing my friend Philip here of paralysis." He stood and continued, "We will be here again tomorrow. We would like to tell you more then." With that Judas stepped down.

Abraham walked up to the dais and asked, "Do you want to hear more tomorrow?"

"Yes," was the response from the congregation.

Aflame With The Spirit: Philip the Evangelist

"Good. So do I. Let us pray: The Lord bless you and keep you; the Lord make his face to shine upon you; the Lord lift up his countenance upon you, and give you peace."

After prayer everyone gathered around Philip and Judas to welcome them and make commentary on Leah's healing and their messages. Soon Abraham said, "We must take Leah home. She's had a full day and may be tired." Philip thought *this man loves his wife just as I loved mine.*

Several people walked with Abraham, Philip, Judas, Elmadam, and Leah as far as their home. Abraham said, "I'd like to invite you in, but we must rest tonight. We'll see you tomorrow. All right?"

"All right, Abraham," someone responded. "You'll see us tomorrow for sure."

The next morning people were standing outside the meetinghouse as Philip and Judas arrived with Abraham, Elmadam and Leah. Abraham said, "Where have all these people come from? We never have more than the place can hold."

As they came closer he recognized some of the people and said, "They're from another meetinghouse clear across town! I wonder what they're doing here."

"Shalom, Abraham! We've come to hear your guests," called one man as he came forward and bowed to greet Abraham.

"Shalom. How did you know I had guests?"

"We had friends come by after your meeting last night. We passed the word that our Sabbath service would be at your meetinghouse today. That is all right, isn't it?"

"Of course. Of course. I hadn't thought about letting you know. I am sorry." Turning to Philip and Judas, he said, "This is my friend Seth."

Philip said, "Shalom, Seth. Thank you for coming and bringing your friends. Judas and I are honored."

The women were talking with Leah, remarking how healthy she looked. She said, "I feel as though I had never been sick."

Abraham said, "Well, let's see if we can get inside," and led the way through the crowd at the door and on to the front of the congregation.

When they stopped, Judas said to Abraham, "Jesus draws large crowds of people everywhere he goes. I should have expected something like this, but it didn't occur to me, either."

Abraham stepped up on the dais and led the chanting of a Psalm. Elmadam read scripture from the Torah. Prayers were said, and then Abraham introduced Philip and Judas, and asked them to tell more about Jesus of Nazareth.

Philip began by reviewing what he had said the night before about John the Baptist, and then about Jesus' healings. He told of his own paralysis, and how Jesus forgave him of his sins. When he heard protests of non-acceptance from the audience, he used the same words Jesus said, "What was easier, to tell me to pick up my bed and walk, or to tell me my sins were forgiven? I needed to be free of the burden I was carrying in my heart before I could be free of my paralysis. The forgiveness was proof to me, and possibly the scribes who were witnesses, that Jesus has an affinity with God that is above the rest of us."

Philip asked Judas to talk, who started by saying, "Abraham, may we sing the Psalm 'The Eternal Dwelling of God in Zion'?"

Abraham came forward and said, "Yes, let us sing."

When they finished, Judas sat on the stool and said, "In this psalm are the words, 'The Lord swore to David an oath from which he will not turn back: "One of the sons of your body I will set on your throne. If your sons keep my covenant and my decrees that I shall teach them, their sons also, forevermore, shall sit on your throne.'" It is my belief that Jesus of Nazareth is the fulfillment of that promise."

"If he's from Nazareth, how can he be from David's line?" came a question from the congregation.

"He was born in Bethlehem, the city of David. He is from David's line."

Murmurs from the crowd were heard. Judas continued with more prophetic scripture that Jesus was fulfilling. Judas seemed to be making Jesus into the warrior-messiah that Philip didn't accept. When he was finished, Philip said to Abraham, "May I talk again? Jesus has taught us so much--we can't possibly tell you everything in one day, but I want to share some of his teachings."

"All right, Philip, for a little while."

Philip went to the dais, sat on the stool and then stood as if changing his mind. He said, "Judas and I have more to share with you than we possibly can in just one day. If we were to stay over another day or two, will you be able to come back?"

"Yes," and "We'll be here," were heard.

"All right, then. We will be at Abraham's house during the day, if any of you want to come see us there, and we will be here again tonight and tomorrow night. Thank you for your welcome. Shalom."

Chapter Six

On the walk home, Abraham said, "I am glad you are going to stay for a few more days. My home is yours as long as you can be here."

Philip said, "Thank you, Abraham. Judas and I haven't had a chance to talk about it yet, but I could see how eager everyone is to learn about Jesus, and we have so much more to tell."

Judas said, "Yes, I was a surprised at your announcement that we would be here after today. We should be starting for Dor tomorrow."

Philip responded, "How can we leave this congregation with the little bit we told them in one day? We have to give them some of his teachings, his strengthening the Law, and making God one of love, not a tyrant."

Judas answered, "I thought I did a good job this morning. Between that and tonight, we could cover the most important points."

Philip snapped, "You were misleading them. You were trying to make him out to be a warring leader, and you know Jesus is not that kind of a person."

Judas retorted, "Not yet! But he told us to preach 'The kingdom of God is near,' and you know what that means--throwing off foreign rulers!"

"No! That is not what it means. You have been with Jesus from the start of his ministry, and you can't get it through your head that God's kingdom is LOVE--not war!"

Abraham said, "I'm glad to hear that. We have too much war and turmoil as it is. A kingdom of love will appeal to the Jews of Caesarea. We try to remain faithful to the Law of Moses, but we do business everyday with people from all over the world. We don't want to suddenly have our business friends become our political enemies. It is hard enough to be Jews in the country of Samaria."

With that they were at Abraham's home. After a light meal, everyone found a place apart to rest. Philip went outside to be in the shade of the house near the garden, and was in private prayer when he heard a knock on the courtyard door. He heard Elmadam greet the visitor, someone he knew, he assumed, as he asked them to enter.

Elmadam came to where Philip was and said, "Will you come in the courtyard? Someone wants to see you."

Philip looked up in surprise. Even though he had issued an invitation, he didn't expect anyone to come on the Sabbath.

As he entered the courtyard through the garden door he saw three adults, two men and a woman, and on a litter was a young boy. Abraham was coming down the stairs, and Judas, already in the courtyard, was getting up from lying on the floor.

Elmadam said, "Philip, these people asked to see you."

Philip's heart immediately went out to the young man on the litter. He greeted the group with a bow of his head and said, "Shalom." Looking at the lad he said, "I see you have need of healing, sir." Placing one hand on the head of the boy and raising the other, Philip looked at him and commanded, "In the name of Jesus, rise and walk!"

The boy, surprised by the suddenness of Philip's action, didn't know quite how to respond. He looked at one of the men for confirmation. Everyone was watching the boy, and the man nodded to him. He made the necessary moves to get his feet under his body. He rose to a standing position. Beaming smiles and laughter exploded from everyone, including Philip.

"Take a few steps," Philip said.

A path was made clear so he could walk around the litter. The woman was weeping and laughing at the same time.

"How do you feel?" Philip asked.

"Strange. It's been so long since I've walked, I'd almost forgotten how."

"I know. It will take time for your full strength to come back, so be careful not to overdo. Understand?"

"Oh, yes." Smiling broadly, the boy came to Philip and almost jumped at him to put his arms around his waist. He said, "Thank you."

Philip could well understand the full range of emotions the boy's mind was traveling through. Yes, indeed! He well understood. He wrapped his arms around the lad's head and gave him a hug.

The man, his face beaming, yet tears were streaming from his eyes, said, "I don't know how we can thank you. It's a miracle. We didn't think he'd walk again."

"Your faith has made him well. Give Jesus the glory. Will we see you at the meeting house tonight?"

"Ah, yes. We'll be there--and all of our friends. We will be there!"

"Shalom," Philip said as he walked to the courtyard door.

"Shalom and thank you again," each one responded as they went through it.

When they were gone and the door closed, Abraham said, "I don't want to sound critical, Philip, but this is the Sabbath. We may be in Caesarea, but we keep the Sabbath holy and do no labor on that day."

Philip looked at Abraham sympathetically, "Do you think healing a paralyzed boy was labor? I did nothing but pray. Jesus' name--and their faith--was the power that healed him."

Judas added, "Jesus told the Pharisees when they made the same kind of remarks that, 'God made the Sabbath for man, not man for the Sabbath.' Then he asked them what they would do if one of their farm animals fell into a well on the Sabbath. Would they leave it there, or would they gather friends and pull it out."

Philip said, "I didn't expect anyone to visit us today, because it is the Sabbath, but when I saw that boy on a litter, it was almost an involuntary reaction to heal him, as we've been trained."

Abraham said, "I understand. I'm so glad you two are going to be here longer than today. I have much to learn."

Chapter Seven

Later in the afternoon another rap sounded on the courtyard door. Again Elmadam answered it. This time it was for both Judas and Philip. Judas, who had been resting in the courtyard with Elmadam, rose to greet the visitors. Philip came into the house.

Standing with Judas in the courtyard were three husky young men, who had the bearing of soldiers, although they were dressed in robes of civilians.

"Shalom," Philip said as he came toward them. "What can we do for you?"

"Shalom," was returned by all three men. One continued, "We were at the meeting house this morning. We wanted to have a private talk with you two."

Elmadam said, "Do you want me to leave?"

"No. We just didn't want to talk with all the people around. You see--we are soldiers

Aflame With The Spirit: Philip the Evangelist

in Herod's guard. We--we knew John the Baptist."

By this time Abraham had joined the group. He said, "Welcome to our home. I am Abraham, and this is my son Elmadam. Will you be seated?"

All three men salaamed to Abraham and Elmadam and said, "Thank you." They sat, cross-legged, on the floor, followed by the four hosts. He continued, "My name is Hasshub, and these are friends."

Judas said, "Tell us, how did you know John?"

Hasshub answered, "We were at Machaerus the ten months he was held prisoner there." Looking down, he continued in a barely audible voice, "We were at the execution." He hesitated. "We took his body--." He was finding it quite difficult to make the words surface through welling emotions.

Philip suddenly felt a revulsion starting in the pit of his stomach and working upward. Gentleness was changing into hatred so quickly! Wishing to lash out at all three men with revenge, he began to shake. He knew he was going to have to hear what these men had to do with John's death.

Hasshub continued, "--and later--the head--to his friends outside the wall."

Philip could hardly hear what Hasshub was saying because of a ringing in his ears. His mouth dropped open and was ready to give them a blistering reprimand they would remember to their dying days.

Just then Hasshub looked up, with tears in his eyes, and said, "We had been students of John for the months we were there by ourselves. We sat at his feet daily." His intake of breath was a sob. He cried, "We loved him! He changed our lives." His companions, sitting with heads bowed, suddenly looked up at Hasshub.

Philip fought for self-control and tried desperately to understand the words being said by Hasshub. He breathed in deeply, and as if by magic, his head cleared. He saw in his mind's eye John standing there in front of him. John had his right index finger to his lips. Philip distinctly heard John say: "Listen to him, Philip. My work was finished. You have three men here wanting to learn more about the Master."

Philip immediately saw Hasshub's need and felt compassion for him. He said, "If Jesus

Aflame With The Spirit: Philip the Evangelist

were here, he would forgive you, as he did me, of the wrong, whatever it was."

Hasshub slowly gained control of his emotions. He looked at Philip and said, "Thank you. We had to tell you this. Please understand, we were under heavy supervision--and had nothing to do with the execution. Nor could we have prevented it. Should we have tried, it would have cost us our lives and gained nothing. This way, we think we may be of service to the Master."

Judas said, "We understand."

After a moment Hasshub said, "We also want you to know barrack gossip has it that Herod thinks your Jesus is John returned. He is aware of the following he is gathering."

Philip inhaled audibly. Judas cleared his throat.

Hasshub continued, wiping his tear-filled eyes with the sleeve of his robe, "We've heard it was the crowds and fear of insurrection that were the real reasons John was arrested."

"Hasshub, I find this to be a difficult moment. Jesus already has the Pharisees, Sadducees and Scribes against him. Now he has Herod to worry about."

Hasshub nodded. "I understand, Philip. John was a very special man. We knew what we were forced to do and we knew we had to share it with you, as unpleasant as it is. Something moved us in this direction so we could tell you."

Philip, once more in control of his emotions, said, "Now that I have the whole story, I can see, so clearly, the hand of the Master at work, which usually means more involvement in the future. Thank you my friend. Thanks to all of you--coming as you have as a group has a great significance--showing your love and sincerity which will certainly be remembered by the Master."

Chapter Eight

That evening, the crowd was bigger than it had been at the morning service. Judas asked Abraham, "Is there a public area nearby we could use? We usually go into the countryside near villages, but the country is too far from here, isn't it?"

Abraham hesitated before answering, "Actually, the outside wall isn't as far as the public square."

Philip said, "Let's speak in the street in front of the meeting house tonight, but tell the people we'll be outside the east gate tomorrow evening. All right?"

Both Judas and Abraham nodded, "All right." Abraham continued, "I'll go in and make the announcement."

In the crowd were many who hoped to be healed of their ailments and illnesses. Judas and Philip went among the people, healing all who asked. After each one, sounds of shouts of praise to God and thanksgiving were heard. They greeted the family of the paralytic who had been made well earlier that day. Hasshub and his two companions were there, too.

When people in homes surrounding the meetinghouse heard the noise from the mass, they came to their doors to investigate. Their curiosity kept them. When they saw what was happening, some went back and brought sick and infirm members of their household. From Philip they also received healing and return of good health. Judas passed them by because they were not Jews.

Eventually Abraham raised his voice and said, "Let's sing a psalm of thanksgiving and praise for sending us these men."

Philip led the teaching, after asking the people to sit, while he stood. He gave them pieces of wisdom he had learned at Jesus' feet. He then asked Judas if he would continue in these teachings, which he did.

Darkness had come over the city, but the people were reluctant to go. Finally, Abraham said, "These men will be outside the east gate of the wall tomorrow evening. They will be at my home during the day. You are welcome to come and see them privately. Go in peace."

Aflame With The Spirit: Philip the Evangelist

Many walked as far as Abraham's house wanting to be near them, watching, listening, and learning as long as they could.

"How much longer do you want to stay here?" Judas asked Philip when they were alone in the courtyard. They were on sleeping pallets given them by Leah.

"I'd like to stay for the entire time. There are more Jews than we expected, and they are so cut off from the rest of us."

"But our destination is Dor. What will we tell the Master?"

"Yes, I agree. We have to go to Dor, but I'd rather remain here. Let's give this place two more days. We haven't even touched on preparation for the kingdom of God. And if we baptize--that will take a whole day."

"Since Caesarea isn't where we were sent, let's not go into either of those subjects. We won't have the time."

"All right, Judas. We'll plan to go to Dor after two days, and while we're here we won't talk about the kingdom of God or baptism. Agreed?"

"Agreed."

Visitors started arriving early the next day. Each one had a special need-- crippled, infirm, or a scholar who desired more information on Jesus' teaching. Judas and Philip worked individually, Judas in the courtyard, and Philip in the garden area in the back of the house. Leah acted as receptionist and host.

Late in the afternoon, she brought to Philip a woman with a small boy. Philip was struck with her beauty. She was tall, nearly as tall as he was, with dark brown hair and eyes. Her sharp features were not that of a Jew-- *probably Greek* he thought as he looked at her.

The child was blind. *He's about the age of my twins*, Philip thought, as he said to him, "Welcome, young sir. May we fix it so you can see?"

The lad responded, "Oh, if you could, my mother and I would be so happy."

To the woman, Philip said, "Are you his mother?" He felt a need to know.

"Yes. My name is Sylvia, and this is Nicholas."

"I'm Philip of Julias. I am happy to meet you Sylvia and Nicholas. I have four daughters. Nicholas, you and my twins are about the same size."

Nicholas asked, "Did you bring them with you?"

"No, they're at home with their grandmother."

"Can they all see?"

"Yes. They can see just as well as you are going to see very shortly."

"Oh, I so hope I can."

"It's wonderful. Here we go." With that he placed one hand over Nicholas' eyes, raised the other upwards and said, "In the name of Jesus, let sight be given to Nicholas." Keeping his hands in those positions for a few seconds longer, he gradually lowered the one upraised, and slightly separated his fingers over the eyes. He felt the boy's body jerk.

"What's happening, Nicholas?"

"I have a pain in my head."

To Sylvia, Philip asked, "Has he ever been able to see?"

"He was born blind."

"Nicholas, daylight is causing the pain. It will take a while for your eyes to adjust to it. Put your hands over mine and I will take mine away. Then you keep your hands there, allowing in the amount of light you can stand. All right?"

Nicholas did as he was told. "All right!"

Sylvia was smiling broadly. *What a beautiful woman*, Philip thought. *I wonder where her husband is.* Out of her mouth as though in answer to his question came, "Your father will be so surprised when he comes home, won't he?"

"Where is your husband?" Philip had a desire to know as much about her as he could.

"Greece. He's a sailor. He should be back within two weeks."

To Nicholas he said, "Can you see your happy mother yet?" Sylvia knelt down to Nicholas' height, and starting to weep with happiness.

Nicholas instinctively put out a hand to "see" his mother, and then realized his eyes were also seeing her. "Oh, oh, Mother--" he was struggling with his new sense, blinking, open-mouthed.

"Nicholas, do you see me?"

"Yes, Mother, I see you. It's wonderful." She grabbed him and held him close, sobbing and laughing.

Nicholas, having a hard time trying to express all kinds of emotion, had a wet face from tears, was blinking at the new world around him.

Aflame With The Spirit: Philip the Evangelist

His mother held him closer, rocking gently to each side.

Philip, grinning, wiped his eyes. He never ceased to be amazed at the power of the Holy Spirit. Mentally, he gave thanks for hearing his prayer.

Releasing Nicholas, Sylvia rose to a standing position and said, "I could almost believe in your God, Philip, after this. Thank you so much. What can I give you?"

"You can come to the meeting tonight outside the east gate and learn more about Jesus."

"Oh, I plan to do that, but I mean a gift, some money, or something for your daughters? This is a wonderful thing you have done for us--giving my son the gift of sight."

"Thank you, but no. I did nothing of my own power. It all came from Jesus. I can't accept anything for something that doesn't belong to me. I am only a channel for his healing power." Philip had never felt more fulfilled than at that moment. He was awed by the way God was working through him on this trip.

That evening outside the wall of Caesarea, the two missionaries told their stories again, and revealed more of Jesus' teachings. Sylvia and Nicholas were there as were Hasshub and his companions and all of the others who had been to the house. The men no longer felt like strangers with so many friendly, familiar faces. Philip had to forcibly keep himself from directing his attention to Sylvia and her happy young son. He was so glad for them both.

The day that followed was of the same pattern, with attendance becoming even larger. That evening, the men told the people they were leaving the next morning to go to Dor.

Philip said, "But we'll be back. We have much more to tell you. Meanwhile, may the Lord God watch between us while we are absent one from another. Shalom."

The next morning as Abraham was ready to leave for his place of business, he said, "Please stop here when you return from Dor. Come for as long as you can, as our guests."

"Thank you, Abraham. Your hospitality has been appreciated," Judas said.

"We'll be back. I have a feeling we'll be visiting Caesarea again and again." Philip added.

Abraham opened the courtyard door. "Come see what awaits you."

Aflame With The Spirit: Philip the Evangelist

They went to the entrance and looked outside. There, patiently waiting, was a line of people with crippled and maimed persons.

Judas said, "We should have left last night by the light of the moon. We'll never get to Dor!"

Philip said, "We have to! Let's go now, and heal these as we leave."

Judas said, "All right. I'm ready."

Goodbyes were said to Leah and Elmadam, and the two missionaries left for Dor, healing as they went.

Chapter Nine

Philip and Judas were seated on the ground, finishing their meal, when Jesus joined them. They were back in camp in the hills outside Capernaum, ahead of the forty days they were given. Some of the others had already returned.

"Judas! Tell me about your trip. What happened in Dor?" Jesus asked.

"We have quite a story to tell. It's hard to know where to start," Judas answered.

"I want to know everything. Hold back nothing. Did you get to Dor?"

Judas said, "Yes, we went to Dor. But we found no one who would give us hospitality, so we went back to Caesarea."

"Caesarea!" Jesus looked away in contemplation for a moment. Philip held his breath. *What would his reaction be*? Then Jesus asked, "What happened in Caesarea?"

Judas hesitated. Philip answered, "Wonderful, exciting things!"

Jesus looked at Philip. "Such as?"

In answer to his question, the men told Jesus of their experience in the city before they left for Dor.

Then Judas continued, "We searched for a place to stay at Dor, but were always turned away. So we decided to go back to Caesarea. It was about two hours away. We knew we'd be welcome at Abraham's. It was evening when we arrived." He continued, explaining each small happening.

As they related the events that followed, they re-lived their return to Caesarea.

Judas had knocked on the courtyard door. Elmadam had answered it, "Judas! Philip! Are we glad to see you again! And so soon! All day people have been coming to the house." Abraham and Leah were behind Elmadam by now and reaching to embrace the men.

"You're just in time for supper. Come and join us," Leah said.

"Thank you, we'd like that," Philip said.

During the meal the events of the day were told. Judas had said to Abraham, "If we can be your guests, we'd like to finish our mission here in Caesarea."

Abraham answered, "It will be our privilege to have you stay as long as you wish."

Philip said, "It will be no longer than four weeks, as we have to allow time to go back to Capernaum. But we'll be able to go into Jesus' teachings about preparation for the kingdom of God and to have a baptismal event."

Abraham had replied, "You men get a good night's rest. Tomorrow Elmadam and I will pass the word that you're back and will be outside the east gate in the evening."

So the healing, teaching and preaching had carried on in the pattern established before the interruption. The crowds grew larger every night. Along toward the end of the four weeks, Philip said to Judas, "Did you have the feeling that some of the people are Herod's soldiers in civilian clothes?"

Judas said, "Yes. They've been with us for quite awhile. We have to be careful not to get political in our remarks, or we'll be arrested."

Philip remembered that he was glad to hear Judas say it, rather than him having to prod Judas to stick to just what Jesus had taught them.

Aflame With The Spirit: Philip the Evangelist

The day of the baptisms had dawned clear and balmy. It was to be in the sea at the beach at the north end of the city, outside the wall. Thousands of people came. Judas and Philip took turns in preaching the message that was first John the Baptist's and then Jesus, "Repent. The kingdom of God is near."

The men had removed their outer garments, walked into the surf to where the water came to their knees. Judas said, "Make two lines. We'll both baptize."

And so it was done. Many were baptized that day, including Abraham, Elmadam, Leah, Hasshub and his companions. Philip didn't voice his thoughts, but he noticed that Sylvia was not among them.

Judas finished their report to Jesus with, "So, a congregation of believers has been established in Caesarea,"

Philip saw how intensely Jesus was listening. Jesus said, "Your report makes me very happy. It is good to have trustworthy people there. I knew you could do it."

Later, after all the missionaries had returned and given their reports, Jesus called them together and said, "I saw Satan fall to earth this day. You have all done well. You have proven to me that you, and people like you, can carry my message to the ends of the world. Your names are written in heaven. Now, I must get on with the duties my Father has given me. We'll visit some of the fellowships you have started. Rest tomorrow. We'll leave for the district of Tyre and Sidon the day after."

Philip spent the next day in Julias visiting his family.

As Jesus and the disciples were returning from Tyre and Sidon, nearing the district of Caesarea Phillipi, north of the Sea of Galilee, they were taking a rest in the shade of some trees near a stream. Jesus asked, "Who do men say that I am?" One answered, "John the Baptist," another, "Elijah," yet another said, "Jeremiah," and other prophets. Then he asked, "But who do you say I am?"

Simon voiced Philip's conviction, "You are the Messiah, the anointed Son of God."

Jesus answered, "Blessed are you, Simon Bar Jonah. God has given you the answer. From henceforth, you are Peter, and upon this rock I will build my church."

Aflame With The Spirit: Philip the Evangelist

A slight frown creased Simon's brow. He said, "I'm just a simple fisherman, Master--I know nothing of how to build Your church."

Jesus replied, "I will give you the keys to the kingdom."

The frown gave way to a slight smile, then a perplexed look as he heard Jesus say, "Whatever you bind on earth will be bound in heaven, and whatever you loose on earth shall be loosed in heaven."

Simon and the others were giving thought as to what those words meant when Jesus added, "Don't tell anyone just yet that I am the Christ."

Everyone fell silent. Here was news that had been foretold and anxiously anticipated for many generations, and they couldn't tell anyone.

Then Jesus said, "I want you to start preparing yourselves. The time is coming when I will be arrested and persecuted, and will be killed."

"No!" Simon Peter shouted, jumping to his feet. "Not You! You can save Yourself from all that."

Jesus replied, also rising to his feet, "You are playing Satan's role, now, and tempting me to forego that which I must endure. Get behind me, Satan!" After pausing a moment He added, "I shall not go into Judea again until my time has come, because when I do I will be arrested. I tell you truly, I will die on the cross."

Philip was stunned at this prophecy out of the mouth of his Master. *If He is to be crucified, what will happen to us, His followers?*

As if reading his thoughts, Jesus said, "If you want to continue following me, you must deny yourself and take up your cross."

Philip had never witnessed a crucifixion, but he knew it was common for the criminal to have to carry the crossbeam through the streets. Certainly at that stage of his life, the condemned man had no choice but to deny himself of everything. *Is that to be my reward for following Jesus?*

Again, Jesus seemed to sense his question. He said, "If you lose your life for my sake, you will gain it. If you save your life, you will lose it."

There He is talking in riddles again! Whatever does He mean?

Jesus continued, "What will you gain, if you win the world, but lose your life?" He looked around at his followers, who were all

Aflame With The Spirit: Philip the Evangelist

on their feet. Everyone seemed as confused as Philip felt. "What will you give in exchange for your life?"

No one ventured to answer.

"You will receive your reward when the Son of man comes with His angels to glorify his Father." After a moment's hesitation, He added, "Some of you who are with me today will yet be alive and see the Son of man coming into His kingdom."

When no one asked what he meant, Jesus said, "Let's be on our way," and they moved on.

About a week later, Jesus took Peter, James and John on a private walk. They were gone most of the day. When at last they returned to camp, and Philip was alone with James, he asked, "Where did you go today?"

James said, "Up on the mountain." They were camped at the foot of Mount Tabor.

Philip asked, "What happened? All four of you have an aura of bright light."

"We can't talk about it. Not yet. And I pray it will be a long time before we can."

"What do you mean?"

James was silent.

"Oh," Philip groaned, "Not that again."

"Yes."

Philip continued following Jesus from place to place all through Galilee. Jesus and a few of his apostles went secretly to Jerusalem to attend the Feast of Tabernacles. Philip spent the time with his family in Julias. When Jesus returned, reports were given of the Pharisees trying to arrest him while he was teaching in the Temple. Philip thought Jesus was fortunate to have escaped, but as he told them, "My time has not yet come."

Chapter Ten

Jesus and His disciples were in the Jordan Valley, near where Philip witnessed John's arrest, when a messenger arrived looking for Jesus. He said, "Mary and Martha of Bethany send greetings. They ask that you come as swiftly as you can. Their brother Lazarus is ill."

Jesus' answered, "He will not die. His illness is for the glory of God. It is the means by which the Son of God will be recognized." Philip saw that he was not eager to depart.

Philip asked Cleopas, another disciple, "Who are Mary and Martha?"

He answered, "Beloved friends of the Master. They and Lazarus, their brother have been supporters of us financially, and when any of us are in Jerusalem, we are always welcome in their home in Bethany."

"I've never been there. How far is Bethany from Jerusalem?"

Vada M Gipson

"Just a few miles. It's on the road from Jericho into Jerusalem."

After two days, Jesus said, "Let's go into Judea again."

His disciples tried to get Him to go under cover of darkness to avoid being stoned. He said, "We can see better during the light of day. I must be in Jerusalem when my time comes."

As they approached Mary and Martha's home at Bethany, Martha saw them coming and ran out to meet them. She cried, "You have come too late. Lazarus died and is in his tomb."

Weeping people were crowded around the house. Philip saw that Jesus had compassion for them, but was not prepared to see Him weep, too.

Jesus said, "He is not dead. He is just sleeping. Where is Mary?"

Martha answered, "I'll run to get her," and took off for the house.

When Mary arrived, Jesus said, "Where is he? Take me to his grave."

Martha said, "But, Lord, he has been there four days. The odor will be foul."

"Nevertheless, show me where he is sleeping," Jesus replied.

Walking up the hill to where some caves were, Philip could see many had large stones covering the entrances. They had been used as graves for generations. All the people were following.

Jesus said, pointing at the grave, "Remove the stone." Several men from among the crowd went to lift away the stone.

Then He raised both hands high toward heaven and said, "Father, thank you for hearing me. I know you do, but these people need to know that you do." Keeping His left hand high, and stretching the right one toward the grave, palm outward, He shouted, "Lazarus, come forth!"

All eyes were on the cave. Philip had been told of other revivals of the dead, but had not witnessed one. And none had been from the grave!

Silence fell on the crowd. Philip found himself holding his breath.

After a few moments, Lazarus, wrapped in burial cloths, appeared at the entrance of the cave. A cheer erupted from the crowd.

"Remove his bonds--set him free," Jesus commanded. Mary and Martha ran to him, untied the scarf covering his head that kept the lower jaw in place, and unwound the cloths binding the remainder of his body. He embraced his sisters.

Many of the people in the crowd fell to their knees. Philip, himself, felt weak from what he had just witnessed. He, too, knelt in awe and adoration. Laughter, praises, and tears of joy were all mixed together.

Lazarus walked to Jesus and started to kneel at his feet. Jesus reached out and embraced him. Lazarus said, "Hello, Master. Thank you for coming." Turning to Martha, he said, "How long have I been gone?"

"Four days. It's a miracle! To have you here, alive, is a miracle!"

"Four days!" Smiling he said, "No wonder I'm hungry--do you have anything for me to eat? I'm starved!"

Both sisters laughed. Martha said, "Come to the house. We'll have a feast!"

Jesus and his disciples remained at Bethany for two days. One of the people who had been present at Lazarus' resurrection came back the next day. Philip heard him say to Jesus, "Some of us who were here yesterday are Pharisees from Jerusalem. When we told our friends about Lazarus, they called you a trouble maker."

When he hesitated, Jesus softly said, "Go on."

"They are planning to kill you--and Lazarus, too."

"Thank you for warning me. My time has not yet come. We must leave here."

So, early the next morning, they departed Bethany and went to Ephraim, a city near the wilderness, about sixteen miles northeast of Jerusalem.

Chapter Eleven

The time of Passover was approaching. Many thousands of country folk went to the Temple in Jerusalem a few days early for purification. Jesus said, "My time has come. We will go to Jerusalem for the Passover." Philip felt a shiver of cold chill pass through him. His desire to see Jerusalem was dulled by a feeling of dread.

They returned to Bethany, to the home of Lazarus, Martha and Mary. Before supper at the home of Simon, a healed leper and a neighbor of Lazarus, Mary brought out a jar of very expensive oil, nard, noted for its fragrance, a product imported from India. She went to Jesus and washed his feet with it, and wiped them with her hair.

Judas, when he saw what she was going to do, said, "Tell her not to, Master. We could sell this oil for a lot of money and give it to the poor."

Aflame With The Spirit: Philip the Evangelist

Philip heard Jesus say, "Leave her alone. She is doing a beautiful thing for me. My body is being prepared for burial. The poor will always be with us, but I will be here yet a little while." Philip's heart sank--he no longer had an appetite for food.

The next day, Jesus called Philip and Cleopas, another disciple, to Him and said, "Go to where the city begins. A young donkey will be tied to a fence. Untie him and bring him to me."

"Master!" Philip said, "That's stealing! We can't do that!"

"If the owner says anything, you tell him your Master has need of it."

"Well," Philip hesitated before finishing with, "As you wish."

As Philip and Cleopas were departing for Jerusalem, Philip asked, "Have you ever been here before?"

"Yes. Many times," Cleopas replied.

"Good, because I haven't."

"My parents live at Emmaus."

"Where is it located?"

"About seven miles the other side of Jerusalem."

As they approached the city wall there stood a house by the road. At the fence of the corral was tethered an ass, a nearly full-grown colt of a donkey, and his mother!

"Look, do you see what I see?" Philip asked.

"You sound surprised, didn't you know we'd find it exactly the way He said?"

"Yes and no. He's always surprising me with his abilities. I am constantly amazed, ever since He came into my life."

As they were untying the colt, the owner came running out of the house. "Hey there! What are you doing?"

Cleopas softly said, "You handle this."

Philip, giving Cleopas a stern look, brightly said, "Good morning sir. Have you heard of Jesus of Nazareth?"

"Jesus of Nazareth?" A puzzled look came on his face. "Yes! He's the one who brought Lazarus back from the dead!" Coming to where they were standing, looking hard into their eyes, he asked, "What about him?"

"We are his disciples. He told us we would find your untrained animal, and to tell you that He has need of it."

"Indeed," he replied. A look of surprised amazement crossed his face. "How did he know it hasn't been ridden? I don't know what good it will be to him, but he is welcome to it."

The men untied the beast as its owner watched. Then he asked, "Is there anything else that I can do for him?"

"Not that we know of. We'll see that you get the donkey back when he is finished with it."

On the way back to Bethany, leading the animal, Philip said to Cleopas, "Have you ridden a donkey?"

"Yes, many times."

"So have I. I'm tempted to let him carry my weight back to Bethany. What do you think?"

"I think you're foolish. This one isn't broken--you wouldn't ride very far."

"I used to be pretty good. When I was little, I used to sit astride the beast."

Cleopas said, "It's a problem now that we're grown and have these long robes around our legs."

Philip stopped and allowed the animal to come alongside him as he said, "I'm going to give it a try."

Cleopas said, "If you do, I'll stand back."

Philip jumped on the back of the colt. No sooner was he on the animal than it sidestepped suddenly, and Philip was on the ground again, in a sitting position. Laughing, Cleopas put his hand out to help Philip to his feet.

He looked at Cleopas with a pained smile. Neither said a word about the incident.

"I wonder what the Master wants him for?" Philip mused out loud.

When Philip and Cleopas had returned with the donkey, Jesus said, "Now I am ready to make my entry into Jerusalem."

Philip said, "I hope you're not planning to ride the colt—he isn't broken. He will throw you as soon as you mount him."

"Don't fret, Philip. Prophecy must be fulfilled, and I must enter riding an unbroken ass." A cloak was thrown over the back of the animal, and Jesus jumped on him. The colt stood steady and docile. Philip was amazed; *even the animals know Jesus is the Messiah.*

Word had spread into the city that Jesus was again at Bethany, and the people poured out of the city to see him and Lazarus. A huge cry of "Hosanna!" arose as he started moving toward the city. Other travelers picked up the shout. Some people broke branches from the trees to lay on the road for the animal to walk upon. Others laid down their cloaks. *What an*

Aflame With The Spirit: Philip the Evangelist

entrance, Philip thought, as he followed along with the other disciples and the multitude. *With this much support from the people, no one would dare try to kill him.* Then Philip remembered that kings and conquering heroes come into cities riding on horses; those who arrive riding a donkey do so in peace. *I hope Judas receives this same revelation.*

They went all the way to the steps of the Temple, where Jesus jumped off the donkey.

What a beautiful building, Philip thought, as he viewed the Temple. Herod the Great had rebuilt it, taking about forty years to do it.

Philip followed Jesus past Roman guards into the Temple. He was unprepared to see that merchants had brought birds and animals to sell to pilgrims for the purification rituals. Moneychangers were there to provide the Tyrian silver coin so taxpayers would have the proper money for the Temple Tax. The moneychangers charged a fee for their service.

Jesus hesitated a few seconds taking in the entire scene. Suddenly, he was upsetting the tables of the moneychangers and the cages of the merchants, shouting, "You are making my Father's house a den of robbers. It is a house of prayer!"

Some of the animals broke loose and were scrambling in every direction. A few birds escaped their cages and were fluttering wildly into the air. Coins were rolling about. The moneychangers were on their knees trying to pick them up. The merchants were tripping over them, sending them sprawling on the floor. Dogs in the nearby area barked. Donkeys brayed and kicked up their heels.

"Go! Leave my Father's house," Jesus shouted. "Your presence desecrates this holy place!" Looking back at the wild man, they hurried away.

This was a side of Jesus Philip had never seen. The loving, gentle Master he thought he knew was furious at those who were destroying the very thing the Temple stood for. He had been told of some of the incidents that had happened in Jerusalem in previous trips involving Jesus' display of temper.

When the area was finally emptied of those Jesus had run out, Jesus stood looking at the scene. He slowly turned, and Philip saw his beloved face wet with tears. Philip's heart was sad as Jesus stood motionless for a few moments, the sound of confusion dying in the background. Jesus looked upward as though silently praying. He seemed to be in deep

Aflame With The Spirit: Philip the Evangelist

thought as He lowered his head. Philip knew the news of this action would spread, and it worried him.

Philip followed along with the other disciples as they went farther into the Temple. Cleopas was by Philip's side. He said, "This is the Court of the Gentiles. Jesus will probably stay here and teach."

And He did. Jesus spent the days healing, teaching and preaching in the Temple. He had a few encounters with the Pharisees and Sadducees testing Him and trying to trap Him. At night, He and some of His apostles went to the Mount of Olives, east of Jerusalem. An olive press was there, called a gethsemane, around which the olive grower had made a lovely garden.

Other disciples went on to Bethany. They stayed with Lazarus and his sisters, and with neighbors. Friends or relatives in the city offered hospitality for the remainder. Pilgrims arriving to celebrate Passover caused much congestion in the homes of villagers surrounding the city. Cleopas asked Philip to go with him to his relatives in Emmaus, which he did.

The day before the Feast of Unleavened Bread, Philip and Cleopas had been healing and teaching in the Temple, as were the other disciples. They saw the apostles Philip and Simon Peter's brother, Andrew, hurrying to where Jesus was. They followed and heard Andrew say, "Some Greeks, who are in Jerusalem for the Passover, want to see you."

Jesus stared at Andrew, as if He were trying to hear something more than the words Andrew had mouthed. He bowed his head and turned slightly and sighed. Then He said, "My time has come to be glorified." Looking around, and seeing that most of His apostles and disciples were within listening range He said, "Remember all that I have taught you. I give you a new commandment: love one another as I have loved you."

Andrew asked, "What shall we tell the Greeks?"

Jesus said, "I am here, and will see anyone as long as I can."

Philip wondered at the significance of the Greeks to Jesus' ominous announcement.

On the first day of Unleavened Bread, when the Passover lamb was sacrificed in remembrance of Moses and the exodus from Egypt, Jesus sent Philip and Judas to prepare the room and meal for him and the apostles.

Aflame With The Spirit: Philip the Evangelist

After entering the city, they met a man carrying a jug of water, just as Jesus told them they would. They followed him to the house he entered. The householder saw them and said, "What do you want?"

"Our teacher said to ask you, 'Where is the room that I am to eat the Passover with my disciples?'" Philip said.

The man squinted as he looked them over, and finally asked, "Who is this teacher?"

"Jesus of Nazareth." Judas answered.

The man seemed to relax, smiled and said, "Follow me." He led them upstairs to a large room. "Here is the room. You can prepare the lamb in the courtyard and bring it up here to eat."

"Do you have the lamb?" Philip asked.

"Yes, I just happen to have one. It's all ready to be slaughtered. Do you want to see it?"

"Yes," both men answered.

The householder led the way back down the stairs and out the kitchen door to the animal pen. Two lambs were penned separately from the others. "Here they are. You can have your choice."

Both disciples examined each animal for flaws. Finding none, Philip said, "Both are in perfect condition. It won't matter which one. Will you have it killed?"

"Yes, I'll take it to the Temple to have it slaughtered and prepare it for roasting. But you have to do the rest."

"That's all right with us." Judas said.

Philip asked, "Do you have enough fuel for the fire, or do we have to get some?"

"There's enough wood, already in the kitchen. My brother and I are going to our parents' for the Passover meal. I didn't know why I was making these preparations."

Judas said, "How much is this going to cost?"

The householder looked shocked. "Cost? How can I charge? After the healing your master gave my brother, whom you followed here, how could I charge?"

Judas said, "Oh! We didn't know, and we don't have too much money, so I had to know what obligation we were getting into."

"No charge. Do you know that the priests called my brother in for questioning?"

Philip, surprised, asked, "What for?"

The man answered, "I think they're trying to find a reason to arrest Jesus. They called in our parents, too. They asked them how long my brother had been blind."

Aflame With The Spirit: Philip the Evangelist

"How long had he been blind?" Judas asked.

"Since birth." He hesitated and then continued with a chuckle, "No, there'll be no charge. I'm just pleased to have Jesus grace my home. He and his disciples are welcome here as long as they need a room."

"Thank you," Philip said. Then added, "Well, we should get ready to roast the lamb. We'll start the fire."

Philip and Judas prepared the Passover meal, including baking the unleavened bread. They carried bowls and cups to the upper room and left everything in readiness. The lamb was finished, but they left it on the stove with a dying fire, and went to the Temple to tell Jesus.

Cleopas had asked Philip to eat the Passover meal with him in Emmaus. As they parted from Jesus and His apostles, they couldn't know the next time they would see Him that He would be hanging on a cross.

Chapter Twelve

Walking from Emmaus toward Jerusalem early the next morning, Philip and Cleopas were heading for Gennath Gate in the west wall near Towers Pool, when Philip spotted an unusual number of people milling around the hill, also known as Golgotha, outside the city wall. "Look! Over there! On Calvary Hill--three crosses--and look at all those people!"

"Let's head for the gate that's nearer the hill. Maybe we'll see someone we know and find out what it's about."

Walking toward the crowd Philip said, "I think I see John--and isn't one of the women Jesus' mother?"

"Yes--yes, I believe it is, and--oh! No!" Cleopas groaned. "God forbid--it can't be—no, it can't be!"

Philip saw it, too. He was stunned at the sight. Their beloved master on the center cross! They broke into a run to where John

Aflame With The Spirit: Philip the Evangelist

and the women were standing near the foot of it. A Roman soldier on duty brought his spear in a forward guard position and challenged the two men, "Halt! Stand there and state your business."

Philip, wild-eyed, responded, "We can't believe what we are seeing. Our friend is on the cross, and we don't know why."

The soldier sized them up, returning his spear to the vertical position, stated as a matter of fact, "Murderers and robbers are the ones who are usually crucified. The sign on the center one reads, 'King of the Jews'."

They both looked at the sign. Philip's heart cried out. The horrible scene drained him emotionally--Jesus, whom he adored, hanging there naked, except for a wreath of thorny bramble bush on his head like a crown. His outstretched arms were pinned to the crossbeam with long spikes driven through them just above the wrists. A crude seat, nothing more than another piece of wood fastened to the cross, provided a bit of resting place for his body. His legs were together, bent at the knees. The feet were one on top of the other. A board sandwiched them to the upright beam with a long spike through the instep area.

Cleopas, completely stunned by the ghastly, terrifying spectacle, bowed his head. Turning it sideways, he closed his eyes tightly as though to block out the sight. He muttered, "Merciful, merciful God, how, oh how can this sort of thing be done? Not one, but three human beings--actually spiked to crosses and left until their life forces literally drain out of their bodies." He began to weep, long, hard, deep emotional, convulsive jerks.

Philip dropped to his knees, completely sickened, staring in shocked disbelief. His chin dropped as he looked at the man up there at his left. Then slowly turning his head, he looked at his beloved master on the center cross before going on to see the man on the right.

His eyes narrowed. A full heavy flush tingled up his spine, up the back of his neck and onto both sides of his face. He mumbled, "What kind of sadistic monster is this ruler--Tiberius Claudius Nero Caesar--who knows this sort of thing goes on?"

The soldier watching the two men said, "Eh? What's that you're saying?"

Philip looked at the soldier in contempt. "Who ordered this awful punishment? Can you tell me?"

Aflame With The Spirit: Philip the Evangelist

"Huh," the soldier grunted, "You Jews amaze me. Who else orders these killings? The Governor of Judea, of course, Pontius Pilate. The one here in the middle brought it on himself."

"What do you mean?"

"He was given a chance to defend himself, but didn't. Even Pilate asked him to speak up in his own defense."

Philip noticed three soldiers over to one side of the crosses casting lots, and it looked like Jesus' robe on the ground. "What are they doing?" he asked.

"Gambling to see who gets his robe," replied the soldier shrugging his shoulder toward Jesus.

Philip placed his hand on top of his head, bringing it down over his forehead, covering his eyes and nose as he started to sob. Anger and depletion of energy fought for supremacy. The sight of this inhuman cruelty was burning deeply into his mind. Jesus' flesh had been cut in a multitude of places. Philip surmised that he had been beaten with whips that had knots or weights.

Just then the Roman leaned on his spear and studied these two men. He asked, suspiciously, "And who might you two be and what is your interest in him?" flipping his head in the direction of the center cross.

Philip sensed trouble, which was something they didn't need. Hoping to appeal to the soldier's vanity he said, "Well, sir--we know him. If you don't have any objection, may we offer our sympathy to the mother standing over there?"

The soldier, sucking in a lung full of air which caused his chest plate to rise, pointed a finger at the two men, said, "Only family is allowed any closer. You stay away."

Philip was relieved to have his attention diverted away from them. Getting to his feet and turning to Cleopas, they turned their backs to the ghastly scene. A few steps away were standing Matthias and Stephen, two other disciples of Jesus, silently weeping.

"Matthias, what happened?" Philip quietly asked.

Matthias and Stephen took them in their arms. Matthias said, "We just came, too. We don't know."

Released from the embrace, Philip looked over the crowd gathered. At one side was a cluster of the apostles, including Peter and Andrew. Judas was standing alone, near them.

Philip said, "Let's go over to the others. Surely someone knows."

Embraces were exchanged as the men greeted each other. Philip noticed that all the apostles looked haggard and weary along with extreme sadness. As Philip embraced Judas he quietly asked, "Do you know how this came about?"

Judas gave him a dark look. "You haven't heard?"

"No. Cleopas and I just now have come from Emmaus where we spent the night," Philip answered. Cleopas, Stephen and Matthias came closer to hear what Judas had to say.

Judas said, "He isn't dead yet. He may yet call on God to send his angels to save him. That will be proof that he is God's chosen one."

Philip felt a cold chill go through his body, as he said, "Judas! Are you responsible for this?"

Judas inhaled, looked down, and mumbled, "At supper last night he told me to do what I had to and to do it quickly." Looking up into Philip's eyes, with tears in his own, he finished, "So I did."

Anger flashed through Philip. Sternly, he asked, "What did you do?"

"I knew the Chief Priests and Pharisees wanted to--arrest him--"

"Yes. We all knew that. Go ahead!" Philip commanded.

"Well, yesterday after we finished preparation for the Passover meal, I made contact with the Chief Priest."

"Judas!" Philip immediately knew his concern for Judas' attitude was justified, and he felt sick at his stomach. He held his hand to his mouth, swallowing hard, fighting the urge to vomit. Gaining control he furiously turned on Judas, "How could you? What kind of a man would do something like that? Didn't you know He would be killed?"

Explosively he answered, "You know as well as I do that Jesus is the Messiah. He can escape from that cross, just by using his power. You know that! I wanted the Chief Priests to know it, too! I wanted an army of angels to come and--and destroy this foreign domination of our country."

Matthias quietly asked, "Did you talk this over with Jesus?"

Judas replied, "No, but He knew. At supper last night He said, 'One of you will betray me.' And when He told me to go ahead, I thought He approved."

Philip's upset stomach again went into a spasm. He turned his back on Judas and walked a few paces away.

Jesus, on the cross, said, "I thirst."

Silence covered the hill as everyone watched a soldier hold his javelin up to his lips. At the tip of the spear was a sponge that had been dipped in vinegar.

Philip couldn't watch his master suffer. He turned and walked back to Judas. "So how did you do it?"

Judas' sorrowful face and contrite eyes showed Philip he was reluctant to have to talk about it. Philip said, "Come on, Judas. What happened?"

"The priests wanted to arrest him at night when people weren't around. I knew He would be in the garden of the olive press for the night. So, I offered to point Him out for their soldiers."

Philip, knowing Judas' need for money, asked, "How much did you charge for this 'service'?"

Hesitating, he finally said, "Thirty pieces of silver." He continued hurriedly, "It was worth it to them. But, if I could undo it, I'd gladly give it back." After a brief pause, he continued, "I didn't think Jesus would allow things to go this far!"

Philip inhaled to speak, but just glared at Judas with tear-filled eyes.

Cleopas spoke for the first time, "Being arrested, and being hung on the cross are two different things. What kind of trial did He have?"

Judas sighed, "It went on all night. The priests took him to Pilate, who couldn't find anything to convict Him of, and sent Him off to Herod Antipas, the Tetrarch of Galilee."

Philip exclaimed, "Antipas! Why?"

"Because Jesus is a Galilean."

Stephen burst out, "So, it was Herod who passed sentence. I'm not surprised. If he could kill John the Baptist, he would kill Jesus."

Judas said, "No, he just sent him back to Pilate. By this time many people were out of bed and in the streets. The priests stirred them up against Jesus. Then they told Pilate the people wanted Jesus crucified."

Cleopas said, "That's not a fair trial."

Judas said, "The Roman Governor traditionally frees a prisoner at Passover. Pilate was willing to free Jesus."

"Why didn't he?" Philip asked in amazement.

Judas continued, "The priests had the people ask for the freeing of Bar Abbas instead."

Philip said, "I never heard of him. Who is he?"

Cleopas answered, "An insurrectionist and murderer." Turning to Judas, he continued, "So, Pilate gave in and condemned Jesus of Nazareth?"

"Yes."

The men were silent, each deep in thought. Philip was thinking: *What happens to the kingdom of God that we preached to be ready for?*

From the cross came, "My God, my God, why have you forsaken me?"

Judas whispered, "Now! Now the angels will come." Everyone watched and waited, but Jesus just remained hanging by the nails through his wrists to the crossbeam.

Gathering dark clouds covered the sun, turning the noon hour into twilight. *Even the sun is ashamed of witnessing this terrible injustice.*

After a half hour of waiting, the apostles joined them. Judas said to them, "I made a grave mistake." Shaking his head, he added, "I am so sorry."

Peter said, "Judas," putting his arm around his shoulder, "I'm unhappy with my behavior, too. I denied being his follower. Not once, but three times! I, who told Him I knew He was the Anointed Son of God said I didn't know Him!"

Andrew said, "Jesus doesn't hold your actions against either of you. His first words from the cross were, 'Forgive them Father, they didn't know what they were doing.'"

Judas said, "He may have forgiven me, but I'll never forgive me." He freed himself of Peter's arm and ran down the hill. They watched him go. Philip worried about what he might do. He was torn between following Judas and remaining with his friends. After a moment of indecision, he said, "I'm going to follow Judas to see that he doesn't harm himself."

Cleopas said, "I'll go with you."

Already Judas was inside the wall of the city, and the two men had to hurry to keep him in sight. They saw that he was headed toward the Temple. Philip said, "We're going to have to get closer. When he gets to the Temple, we'll lose him for sure."

Aflame With The Spirit: Philip the Evangelist

So they quickened their pace to a run. When Judas reached the Temple, he went directly to the priests' chamber. Philip and Cleopas arrived just in time to hear him say, "Here is your blood money! I'm sorry that I fell for the temptation. Here! Take it!"

"We can't take the money back. It's yours. You earned it. Go buy yourself some land with it," one of the priests replied.

Judas threw the thirty pieces of silver on the floor. The coins were still rolling and clinking as he turned away. He almost bumped into Philip and Cleopas. "What are you two doing here?" he yelled.

Philip said, "We felt that you might need us. Let's go somewhere and talk."

Judas hesitated then said, "You can do something for me. I don't want to be responsible for the treasury any more." Reaching inside his robe, he produced a heavy pouch. Handing it to Philip, he said, "You can take it to Peter for me, if you will."

"We'll take it, but we don't want to leave you in your present state of heart-break," Philip answered.

Judas looked at Philip as though he was surprised at his concern for Judas' well being. "I'll be all right. I'm going out to the garden of

Gethsemane--to pray. You take the money and go back to Calvary."

Philip looked at Cleopas questioningly. Cleopas shrugged his shoulders. Turning to Judas he asked, "Will you promise that you'll meet with us in the upper room for the Sabbath?"

Judas mumbled, "I may be there but--I won't promise." He turned away seemingly determined to get away by himself, and started walking toward the Golden Gate, the one nearest the garden. Philip and Cleopas watched him go, turned and retraced their route back to the Hill of Calvary.

About three hours after the clouds came over the face of the sun, Jesus whispered, but clearly enough to be heard by the waiting crowd, "It is finished."

Immediately the earth shook violently. People lost their balance and fell to the ground. Philip expected to see walls and buildings collapse, it was so strong. And some did. When it was over, the sun broke forth in its full mid-afternoon glory. Philip felt awed by the power of the spiritual realm manifesting itself in their presence.

Aflame With The Spirit: Philip the Evangelist

About an hour before sunset, the beginning of Sabbath, Philip heard pounding. He turned to see soldiers break the bones in the legs of the one on Jesus' right with a heavy club. When they came to Jesus, one of the soldiers said, "This one is dead already."

The other replied, "I'll stick my spear in his side, just to be sure." As he did, blood and fluid drained out of Jesus' body. "Now we know. He's dead."

Philip noticed the soldier that pierced Jesus side was wearing His robe. He couldn't watch any longer and turned away. He heard the soldiers pounding the legs of the third one. Many times he had heard of the sickening atrocities performed by the Roman soldiers, but to witness them was repulsive beyond belief.

When he was able to speak Philip asked Cleopas, "What's the reason for breaking their legs?"

Cleopas answered, "They know the Jews don't want the bodies up there on the Sabbath, so they break the legs to speed their death. Then they can be taken down before sunset."

"All of this is so sickening. I've never seen this kind of cruelty before. How does breaking their legs hasten their death?"

"When the legs are broken, the body's weight hangs just by the arms. They can't breath and they suffocate. It's a quicker, but a more painful death."

They won't even let a person die without making it more painful. Aloud he said, "I can understand why our forefathers thought crucifixion was the most disgusting form of death." Pausing in thought, he added, "But we know Jesus was not accursed by God!"

"Yes, we know. It was the ruling priests that brought about Jesus' being up there."

Two men with several servants came up the hill toward the captain of the guard. Pointing at them, Phillip asked Cleopas, "Do you know who they are?"

Cleopas gasped and replied, "Yes! That's Joseph of Arimathea, and Nicodemus, two Pharisees. Let's get a little closer and see what they want."

So they followed them to hear what they had to say.

Joseph said, "Our Sabbath is beginning soon. We have Pilate's permission to receive Jesus' body. Would you have your soldiers remove it from the cross?"

The captain replied, "Do you have it in writing?"

Aflame With The Spirit: Philip the Evangelist

"Yes." And he produced a small scroll.

Before looking at the decree, the officer asked, "Where are you going to take it?"

Joseph stiffened to have to explain his plan to the officer. "It's all in the order you hold in your hand."

The captain, while glaring at the man, unrolled the scroll, glanced at it, rolled it up and kept it. Philip thought: *he can't read*!

"Guards!" The captain called, "Haul down the one in the center. These men are going to take the body. Two of you stay with them, and remain at the grave until you're relieved."

As soon as the cross was lowered, the long nails removed from wrists and feet freeing the body from the cross, the two men set about preparing it for burial. Nicodemus had brought about a hundred pounds of myrrh and aloes, along with linen cloths. After the body was prepared, they and their servants carried it to a new, unused tomb just below the hill. The family followed, as did Philip with the rest of the disciples and apostles who had kept a vigil all day.

After the body was placed in the cavern, the two soldiers pushed a huge boulder in place to cover the entrance. Then they drew sticks to determine who would stand guard.

The other went off a short distance to a garden nearby to take leisure. The sun was beginning to set.

John said to Peter, "James and I will go with the women to Lazarus' home in Bethany, then we'll meet you in the upper room where we ate last night. We should be safe there."

Chapter Thirteen

Philip and Cleopas went with the others to the house of the upper room. Judas never came. Philip gave the purse to Peter and told him of his worry about Judas. When John and James returned from Bethany, John said to Philip, "Judas has killed himself!"

"Oh, no!" Philip put his hand to his mouth. "Where? How?"

"As we were taking the women to Lazarus' house, we were going up the Mount of Olives. Some soldiers were taking his body to bury it in a potter's field."

"And you saw the body--you're sure it was Judas?"

"Yes. I saw the body."

Philip sighed, "I was afraid he'd do something like that. I've had my experience with guilt, and know how devastating it can be. I'm sorry that I couldn't help him."

John said, "You knew him better than the rest of us. Why do you think he betrayed Jesus to the priests?"

Philip looked at the floor, giving thought to his answer. Finally he said, "Judas was expecting a Messiah as another King David, or Judas Maccabeus, not the non-violent person we knew Jesus to be. He wanted so much for Jesus to be what he, Judas, was awaiting that he forced Jesus into the position of losing his life or proving himself to be the Son of God he was looking for."

John said, "We heard Jesus tell him to do what he had to and do it quickly. Have you any idea why Jesus would give him permission? All of us know that Jesus could read our thoughts."

"I don't know. I just don't know. Jesus has been warning us that He was going to have to die. Perhaps Judas' betrayal was part of an over-all plan."

John said, "Well, I don't suppose we'll ever know."

The Sabbath and next night were spent in prayer and meditation on what the future held for them. They supported each other in their grief and fear of remaining in Jerusalem. Just

Aflame With The Spirit: Philip the Evangelist

being a Galilean was risky. The priests knew their accent.

As time brought dawn near, Philip said, "Before going back to Bethsaida, I want to go to Caesarea once more. The congregation there needs to know what has happened."

Cleopas said, "I'll go with you."

"Would you, Cleopas? I'd like that. How soon shall we leave?"

"I'm ready whenever you are. We can travel by way of Emmaus. I'll get some things from home."

The sound of someone knocking on the courtyard door caused a quietness to settle in the room. The householder allowed the person to enter. A light knock on the locked door to the upper room was heard, and a woman's excited voice saying, "Let me in. Our Master has risen."

The door was hurriedly unlocked and swung open. Eager to enter was Mary of Magdala. Her beaming smile seemed to brighten the twilight of the early morning hour.

Peter asked, "What do you mean 'risen'?"

Entering, Mary said, "Four of us went to the grave at dawn with spices. We intended to

Vada M Gipson

ask the guard to let us in to put them on Jesus' body." She hesitated with excitement.

"Yes? Yes, Mary. What happened?" John asked.

"The stone was already rolled away, and the body--gone! The body was gone! At first I thought it had been stolen." Her eyes suddenly grew large as she related, "As I was looking inside, two men in dazzling white garments were by my side."

When she hesitated, John impatiently said, "Oh, Mary! Please."

"One of them said, 'Why do you look for the living among the dead? He is not here for He has risen. Don't you remember that He told you that He must die, but He would return in three days?'"

Peter said, "This I have to see for myself." And he shot through the still open door and ran downstairs.

"I'm going, too," John added, as he followed Peter.

Mary said, "I'll go with you," and she ran down the steps behind John.

Philip looked at Cleopas and said, "It can't be true. We'd better be on our journey, don't you think? We have a long way to travel."

Aflame With The Spirit: Philip the Evangelist

Good-byes were said to the other followers of Jesus. Philip and Cleopas departed. As they walked along they reviewed the events beginning with Jesus' triumphant entrance into the city. They told each other bits of information they had heard of happenings in their absence.

Without realizing anyone else was on the road, suddenly a man was walking beside them. Philip's heart leapt in his chest, yet he didn't feel fearful. The man asked, "What is it you are talking about?"

Surprised to have a stranger join them, and then to have him ask such a question, Philip asked, "Where have you been that you don't know what has been happening?"

The man said, "I am just curious. Tell me."

So Philip and Cleopas, in answering the man's question, reviewed the events that were still so fresh in their minds. Cleopas stated, "Some women even thought they saw angels this morning, telling them He had risen from the dead!"

The stranger chided them, "Why can't you believe it? All the prophecies have been fulfilled!" Starting with Moses, he brought to their attention all the things Jesus had done.

Philip and Cleopas exchanged glances. Philip felt he was having a mystical experience. When he would turn to look at the stranger or to ask him who he was and where he came from, his thoughts would become confused, and he'd drop the question.

When they reached Cleopas' family home, it being about the noon hour, Cleopas asked the stranger, "Will you join us for a meal?"

He replied, "Thank you. I shall."

Cleopas opened the door to the courtyard of his home and called, "Mother. I'm here with Philip and a guest."

A woman's voice answered, "Welcome, son. Help yourself to the bread and cheese."

The men bathed their hands and faces. Cleopas brought the food to the table, and gave bread to the guest to break. He raised it with both hands and prayed.

Immediately Philip and Cleopas saw the man was no stranger. He was their beloved Master, Jesus! Philip almost choked from deep emotions brought to the surface. Tears started to flow from both disciples' eyes, mixed with a desire to laugh. When they reached to embrace Him, a snap occurred as though a stray lightning bolt had entered the room, and

Aflame With The Spirit: Philip the Evangelist

He was gone, disappeared, leaving Philip and Cleopas staring incredulously at each other.

"We must tell the others! Jesus isn't dead!" Philip fairly shouted. They jumped up from where they were sitting at the table, and almost ran back to the upper room in Jerusalem.

The door was locked. Philip and Cleopas pounded on the courtyard door. Eventually a cautious voice from inside asked, "Who is it?"

"Philip and Cleopas. We must come in!"

A relieved householder opened the door, salaamed to the men as they entered. They were physically tired but stimulated by their revelation. Politely, but quickly they returned the courtesy of the ceremonial bow. "Thank you," Philip said. Then asked, "Are the others upstairs?"

"All but one, Judas Iscariot, I think he is called, the one who helped you prepare for the Passover meal. Go on up to them."

Philip and Cleopas raced up the steps. The door to the large upper room was closed and locked. Cleopas knocked and called, "Peter, we are Cleopas and Philip. We have great news. Let us in." Someone opened the door to admit them to the large room, which was as big as the ground floor of the building.

Philip was surprised to see his grief-stricken friends to whom he had said good-bye just a few hours before now showing another kind of expression. And he was stunned to see Jesus' brothers James and Jude in the midst of the apostles and disciples. They, who tried to dissuade Jesus from his ministry of healing, teaching and preaching, were here! Had they also heard the good news?

"Peter!" Philip called, "We've seen the Master! He lives!"

Peter came quickly saying, "I have seen Him, too, and so has his brother James! Where did you see Him?"

Philip and Cleopas told of their experience. Then Peter said, "Mary Magdalene also saw Him."

"So she really did see Him?" Cleopas asked.

"I couldn't believe her, but what she told us this morning was fact," Peter answered.

The Apostle Thomas said, "I think all of you saw someone who resembled Jesus. He died on the cross. We saw the soldier pierce His side with his spear."

Philip looked at Cleopas, then almost shouted at Thomas, "We saw Him! He walked

Aflame With The Spirit: Philip the Evangelist

with us, and talked with us, and broke bread with us. We know what to think! He lives!"

Thomas said, "I'm going to the grave to see for myself."

Peter said, "Go, Thomas. Come back and tell us what you see."

Thomas left the group and went down the stairs. The door closed and James locked it.

At that moment, Jesus was standing in their midst.

"Master! You are alive!" John exclaimed, as he went to his knees. The others jumped back in fright, except Peter, Philip and Cleopas, who knelt in adoration.

"Don't be afraid," He said to the ones who had not yet accepted what they were seeing. "Shalom. If you doubt, look at my hands and feet. Touch me. Ghosts don't have flesh. It is me, and I would like something to eat."

They scurried around and prepared a meal. While Jesus ate, He reminded them of the things He had said was going to happen to Him. As He spoke, Philip's memory confirmed that which He said. Jesus had prophesied all that had happened, including His resurrection. Philip had not been able to comprehend before because he couldn't face the possibility of Jesus' death.

Jesus said, "As I have been sent, I now send you." He walked to each man and breathed on him. "Receive the breath of my spirit. You are part of Me. If you forgive the sins of anyone, they will be forgiven." And then He was gone, vanished. The disciples were left, dumb-founded, looking at one another.

They jumped when a knock sounded on the door. It was Thomas, returning from his quest.

Peter said, "You just missed Him, Thomas. He was here with us, but just left."

Thomas, frowning, said, "I met no one going out. How could He have just left? I can't believe it--I won't believe it--unless I see Him for myself, and see His hands and feet."

"You may have your chance. We are to remain here for the time being," John replied.

"I would love to see him again," Thomas said.

Thomas had his chance seven days later. Many of the disciples and all of the apostles were gathered in the upper room, Philip and Cleopas among them. They were commemorating the event of seeing their risen Master a week earlier, following the example He had given them at the apostles' last supper

Aflame With The Spirit: Philip the Evangelist

with him. They were eating the broken loaf of bread in memory of His body, and drinking wine from the cup in memory of His spilled blood while on the cross. The joy of seeing Jesus had faded the sadness.

Suddenly, Jesus was in the room with them. Immediately Philip felt the air charged with energy, each man jumping to his feet.

Jesus said, "Shalom. Don't be afraid. Remember, I told you that when two or more are gathered together in my name, I am there. And I will be always, even when you can no longer see Me."

Holding out his arms toward Thomas He said, "You wanted to see for yourself? Blessed is the person who believes without seeing!"

Thomas knelt and said, "My Lord and my God! Forgive my doubting."

Philip thought: *All of us are like Thomas. We had to see for ourselves to really believe the Master had risen from the grave.*

Jesus stayed and reviewed much of His teachings, encouraging and preparing His followers to carry on His work. Philip understood everything so much better, and he felt the others did too. It was as though their minds had been opened to receive knowledge where a curtain of fog had existed.

Vada M Gipson

Just before Jesus disappeared He said, "Wait for me in Jerusalem."

Chapter Fourteen

Why had the apostles given up the hope and expectation of seeing Jesus once more? Jesus had asked his disciples to wait for him in Jerusalem. These thoughts were among many that Philip had on the way to Galilee.

They took the route through Jericho and up the Jordan Valley. He reviewed in his mind the whole experience with Jesus, wondering if, indeed, it was all over. *I am not ready to resume life without being involved with Jesus' ministry in some way. At the same time I doubt my own ability to carry on Jesus' work.* More than a few had expressed feelings of not being fit, although most of the disciples had elected to wait in Jerusalem. At times Philip, too, wished he had waited. At one moment his pride would be challenged by the thought of being one of those who extended Jesus' teachings to more people. At another, thinking: *Who am I to represent Jesus, the Messiah?*

When they reached Capernaum, those who lived in that village went to their homes. Philip and a few others went to Julias via Zebedee's fishing boat. It had been a month or more since Philip had seen his family. His twin daughters were eight years old, Ruth was six, and Esther four.

As Philip approached Ishi and Zipporah's home, where his children were living with their dead mother's parents, the door of the courtyard flew open and through it came four little girls running to meet their father.

"Daddy! Daddy! We know you'd come today!" was shouted to him as they ran toward each other. He thought: *I'll never be able to surprise my daughters. They are still little prophets.*

Stopping, squatting down, he embraced them, marveling at their growth. Carrying Esther, the youngest, and taking Ruth's hand in his, they went to the house, where Zipporah was waiting in the courtyard door.

He put Esther down, and took Zipporah in his arms. It seemed as though years had passed instead of the month since leaving them. Suddenly Philip felt old and tired.

Aflame With The Spirit: Philip the Evangelist

Zipporah said, "Ishi will be home soon for our first meal. Will you stay?"

"Yes, Mother, thank you. I need to hear how my girls are doing and catch up on events around here."

"We've heard about Jesus being crucified. We're so sorry. All of us thought for sure that he was the Messiah."

Philip, placing his hands on her shoulders and looking directly into her eyes, solemnly replied, "He IS the Messiah, Mother. He rose from the grave and lives. I've seen him and have talked with him. He really lives!"

Zipporah half opened her mouth with a little gasp and stared unbelieving at Philip. It was not proper for a woman to question or contradict a man's statement, so she said no more.

Prisca, one of the twins, said, "I told you, Grandmother, didn't I? Jesus would die, but he would return. Didn't all of us tell you?"

"Yes, my dear, you did, but you don't know how hard that is to believe!"

Philip said, "Believe it. What I have seen is incredible, I must admit. But I know what I have witnessed."

Just then Ishi entered the courtyard, and shouted, "Philip! How good to see you again!"

Then soberly, he commented how sad he was to hear of Jesus' death--and on the cross, the most shameful kind of death according to the scriptures.

Philip told of his experience on the road to Emmaus with Cleopas, concluding with, "And He came among us as we waited in the upper room where He had eaten the Passover meal. He was not a ghost, nor a spirit. He ate with us and drank with us. He truly lives!"

Ishi looked askance at Philip. He seemed relieved to change the subject as Zipporah brought food to the courtyard table. Philip learned about events that had happened in his family and in the village. He said, "I haven't become accustomed to Bethsaida's name being changed to Julias."

Ishi said, "Here's something else that will take a lot of getting used to. Our ruler, Herod Philip, has married Herodias' daughter, Salome!"

"No!" Philip frowned, reviewing the events of the past. "Not the one who danced for John the Baptist's head?"

"The same! And they spend most of the year right here at his palace in Julias. She is a beautiful young woman. Sometimes we see

Aflame With The Spirit: Philip the Evangelist

them as they come and go. I just heard that he has not been well lately."

Philip thought, *Oh! The wasted lives of those who live only for their own desires, by the labor of others.* Aloud he said, "That kind of living is not for me. Serving Jesus, the Christ, is much more challenging and rewarding." Reaching over to place his hand on Ishi's shoulder, he continued, "Thank you, Ishi, you've helped me to make up my mind."

Ishi tilted his head slightly as he looked at Philip and slowly said, "I don't understand. What do you mean?"

Philip hesitated. He looked at his daughters and at his mother-in-law, Zipporah. Searching for the right words to explain what was on his heart, he began, "Dear ones," taking a deep breath continued, "Jesus commissioned us to take His message into the world. I have had feelings of unworthiness, and questioned my abilities."

When he paused, Ishi softly said, "So you've come to a firm decision?"

"Yes. Whatever lies ahead, I know I can trust in Jesus. He told us, 'Whatever you pray for you shall receive, if you believe.' I feel confident that wherever I am sent, He will be near."

Phoebe said, "Abba, may we go with you? We can help."

Philip, unprepared for this request, answered, "I don't know what the future holds." Teasingly, he added, "I should be asking you about the future. You are always telling me."

Prisca, soberly said, "We know you will be living near the sea for a long time."

Ceasarea immediately came to Philip's mind. Alertly and seriously Philip asked, "Which sea, Prisca? Galilee?"

"It's not Galilee," Prisca replied.

"It's a big, big sea. And you're going to have a big house there," Phoebe added.

"What else about our future do you know?"

Prisca said, "We don't know if we are there with you."

Sighing, and looking lovingly at his children, who were serious in their hope to be with their father, he said, "When I am living in that big house, I'll send for you. That I promise."

Wreaths of smiles brightened four young faces. Even Zipporah, Ishi and Philip, caught-up in the moment, joined them in their happiness.

Aflame With The Spirit: Philip the Evangelist

After the meal Philip and the girls went to greet Philip's parents, Jacob and Mary, his brothers and their families. He re-told the story of Jesus' resurrection. He finished by saying, "I must tell Simon Peter that I'm returning to Jerusalem to wait as Jesus asked us to do." Turning to Nathaniel, his fisherman brother, he asked, "May I go out with you tonight and be left at Capernaum tomorrow morning?"

"Of course," Nathaniel responded.

"So soon?" responded his mother and daughters.

"Yes. I may be too late, as it is. Jesus asked us to wait for him in Jerusalem. After a couple of weeks with no more visits from him, the apostles decided to return to their nets."

Not one of the boats caught any fish that night. Philip was able to sleep the whole night without being awakened to help haul in the net. Dawn found them near the shore not far from Peter's boat. A solitary man had a fire started on the beach. He called, "Peter, how many fish have you caught?"

Peter shouted back, "Not a one."

The man yelled, "Cast your net out the other side of your boat."

Philip stared at the figure on the shore. It was still too dark to make out features, but his form looked familiar.

Nathaniel said, "If casting the net on the other side will help Simon to catch fish, we may as well try it, too."

Philip gave a hand in bringing the net into the boat, and throwing it out the other side. Within five minutes the bell rang alerting them to a full net! Philip could see activity on the other boats indicating the same had happened to them.

Philip stripped himself of his clothing as did Nathaniel and his helper as was the custom when they worked on the boat. After they had pulled aboard the net full of fish, Nathaniel said, "I've never had a net this full without it breaking. Something mysterious is going on here."

At that moment they heard John shout, "It is the Master!" Then they saw Simon Peter hurriedly putting on his clothes. He jumped into the water and swam ashore. The others brought the boat to shore, but it was slow going. They had been unable to lift their net, it was so full of fish.

Aflame With The Spirit: Philip the Evangelist

Clearly, they heard Jesus' voice as He said, "Bring some of your fish and have breakfast with me."

Philip said, "I must go ashore, too!" and started putting on his clothes.

Nathaniel maneuvered his boat close enough for Philip to wade ashore. Philip turned to embrace his brother and crewman before leaving, saying, "I am so happy this has happened, so you also can be witnesses to the risen Lord!"

Nathaniel said, "I can not deny what I see with my own eyes."

As Philip approached the group he saw apostles Peter, Andrew, Thomas, John and James. They were so intent in greeting the master that they paid no attention to Philip, which was all right with him. He just wanted to gaze once more on his Master.

After breakfast, Jesus seemed to center on Peter. Three times he asked Peter if he loved Him. After Peter affirmed that he did, Jesus would say, "Feed my sheep." Peter became perturbed that He was asked three times the same question. Philip remembered Peter's confession on Calvary Hill that he had denied knowing Jesus, not once, but three times. He wondered if Peter realized that he was being given penance for each denial.

After breakfast Jesus said, "Return to Jerusalem for Pentecost, and wait for me there. I will send you a Comforter." And He disappeared before their eyes.

The seven looked at one another as if to confirm that the others had also witnessed what each had seen. Peter said, "We must return to Jerusalem."

They boarded Peter's boat and sailed to Capernaum to start their journey.

Chapter Fifteen

The apostles and disciples were devout Jews. As such they stopped their activities to pray at the third, sixth, and ninth hours. They felt God heard their prayers wherever they were, but when they could go to the Temple in Jerusalem they felt closer to God. They continued to observe the ritual of prayer and, since they were in Jerusalem, they went to the Temple.

After their return from Galilee, as they finished their praying on the fortieth day since Jesus' resurrection, they were aware that Jesus was in their midst. Philip heard him say, "Follow me." His heart replied, *"Anywhere, dear Lord,"* but his mouth kept silent.

Jesus led them out through the Golden Gate and toward the village of Bethany. On the way He reminded them of the prophecies that had been fulfilled. Someone asked, "Are you going to restore the kingdom to Israel?"

Philip thought: *they'll never learn that the kingdom Jesus preached is not an earthly one.* Then he heard Jesus answer, "It is not for you to know God's schedule. But wait in Jerusalem. A Comforter will be sent. John baptized with water, but you will be baptized with the Holy Spirit. You will be My witnesses in all of Judea, in Samaria, and in all of the world. Wait in Jerusalem."

As they reached the summit of Mount Olive, Jesus stopped, turned, raised his arms, and said, "God bless you, my children." He walked a few steps. Philip and the others were ready to make a first step to continue following Him when He was lifted from the ground and a misty cloud formed around him and carried him upward, away from them.

They stood, fixed in their places, staring at the vacant sky where he had been. Suddenly two men in white robes were with them. One said, "People of Galilee, why do you stand here looking into air? This Jesus, whom you just watched ascend into heaven, will return the same way." And then they were gone.

Philip said to Cleopas, who was standing next to him, "Did you see what I did?"

Cleopas replied, "It's hard to comprehend. We'll see him again, but I wonder when."

Aflame With The Spirit: Philip the Evangelist

"It won't be long. There's no doubt. We'll wait in Jerusalem for His Comforter, whoever that may be. But I'm at the point where nothing can surprise me. It's unbelievable what has happened!"

In Jerusalem, the eleven apostles and many disciples were in the upper room where Philip and Judas had prepared the Feast of the Passover for Jesus. The house was located in a section of Jerusalem known as the Essene quarter. They were sitting eating a meal. Also among them were Jesus' mother, Mary, and his brothers. Before breaking the bread and drinking the wine they had remembered Jesus' words at their last supper together, "As oft as you do this, do it in remembrance of me."

Looking into the faces of those assembled, Peter said, "We must select an apostle to replace Judas Iscariot."

John, rubbing his chin with thumb and forefinger, asked, "How shall we go about it?"

Running his tongue along his upper lip, then the lower one as though trying out the words in his mind, Peter slowly answered, "I've been praying about it, and this is what

I've received. He must have been one of us from the beginning."

Philip observed soft murmuring among the disciples. He leaned near Cleopas and said, "That lets me out."

Cleopas replied, "Me, too."

Matthew said, "We have two who have been faithful followers since Jesus was baptized."

"Who are they?" Peter asked.

"Matthias and Joseph Bar Sabbas."

Peter thought for a moment then said, "Both worthy men. Let us pray: Lord, you know the hearts of us all. Which of these two men shall we name to be an apostle in your ministry?"

After a moment's silence, John said, "We should cast lots."

Peter said, "What shall we use?"

John asked of the assembly, "Does anyone have a stone in your purse?" He knew that some people believed special stones had healing properties. Two individuals produced coin-size stones. Giving them to Matthew, John said, "Mark one for Matthias and the other for Joseph." Matthew did so, and handed them back to John, who placed them in a cup and raised his arm, swirling the cup in his hand. One stone flew out, landing on the table, rolling a distance and settled. "Matthias!" several men called.

Peter called Matthias from among the disciples, and space was made for him to sit with the apostles. Peter said, "Bring a basin and a towel."

When the asked-for articles were given to Peter, he knelt before Matthias and put his feet in the basin. As he was drying them Peter said, "Matthias, you have been with us from the beginning; you were here when we witnessed the Lord's resurrection. God bless you in your ministry."

Matthias softly said, "It is an honor and privilege to sit among you. I pray for your patience and understanding as I move into this position of responsibility." He looked into Peter's eyes, looked at his washed feet and back into Peter's eyes. "Tell me, why did you wash my feet?"

"The night of our last supper with Jesus, he insisted on washing our feet. He said, 'If I do not, you can have no part of me.' So, I am making you a part of us and part of Jesus, too."

A smile came over Matthias face. Placing a hand on Peter's shoulder, he said, "Thank you, dear Peter. Thank you."

A moment of reverent silence was upon the gathering. Then John said, "If you have need of more of His teachings, any one of us will be glad to relate them to you."

Jesus' brother James said, "My brothers and I have need. We want to become part of His ministry, too."

Praises to God were heard from the apostles. Peter said, "Before we were sent out two-by-two, we were given an intense class in what to say and how to heal. We will need to review, so we will begin our studies today."

John said, "We found that small groups work better than large ones for something like this."

"That's right, we did," Peter responded.

So the ten days passed until Pentecost, between prayer times, as the apostles and disciples in groups of ten recalled the teachings Jesus had given them. Philip was in the group led by James, John's brother. He noticed the other James, Jesus' brother, was in Matthew's group.

One afternoon Philip reminded James, the apostle, of the incident in the mountains near

Caesarea Philippi when he had gone for a walk with Jesus and something happened that he couldn't yet talk about. He asked, "Can you tell us about it now?"

James' face lit up. He said, "Yes! We went up the mountain, to the top. While we watched, Jesus' clothes became radiantly bright and his face shone. Two men appeared with him, and we recognized--I don't know how--we just knew they were Moses and Elijah. They were brilliantly lighted, too."

One of the group asked, "What happened?"

"Well, Peter said, 'It is good that we came, Master. We should commemorate this day by building three shelters. One for each of you.' Just then we heard a strong voice coming from a bright cloud overhead--"

Someone gasped. James continued, "--Yes, really! It came from a cloud overhead, and it said, 'This is my Son, with whom I am well pleased. Pay attention to what he says.'"

When James paused, Philip was aware everyone in the room was listening. Silence enveloped them; no one wanting to stop the revelation of this sacred event.

"We were awe-struck. We knelt and put our faces to the ground. Jesus said, 'Don't be afraid. Rise!' And when we looked, he was there by himself, his clothes looking normal. Then he told us not to tell anyone until after he had been raised from the dead."

Philip said, "I remember when you returned to camp, all of you were glowing. Did Jesus say anything else?"

James said, "Yes, John asked him about the Scribes saying that Elijah must come first, and he said, 'Elijah has already come, and people have killed him, as they will kill me.' We perceived that he was meaning John the Baptist and his death."

A flash of memory brought Philip back to the first time he had met John the Baptist, and how he thought of Elijah and wondered why. So! John was Elijah returned. John probably didn't realize it himself, but Jesus did.

On the Day of Pentecost, the householder led them to a large synagogue used by the Essenes. It was festival time when the winter barley had been harvested, and "first fruits" were brought to the temple. The city streets were crowded with Jews who had made the trip from all over the known world to Jerusalem for the holiday.

Aflame With The Spirit: Philip the Evangelist

Peter, who loved to sing, opened the celebration with the chanting of some of the praise psalms. After prayers of thanksgiving, he asked of the other apostles, "Do you remember the prayer Jesus taught us?"

Matthew said, "Yes. I'll refresh your memory. Repeat after me, 'Our Father in heaven, holy is your name.'" And Matthew went all the way through the Lord's prayer.

Peter began to speak. A role he had never before taken.

Suddenly a sound of rushing wind filled the meeting place. Philip, who was seated next to Cleopas, felt a flush of heat throughout his body. It was like that which he experienced when he was healed of his paralysis, except warmer. He felt moved to praise the Lord, but when he opened his mouth strange words came out. He closed his mouth, trying to figure what was happening. He tried it again. The same thing happened. He turned to Cleopas, who was experiencing the same thing.

Peter began to speak in a foreign language, then Matthew, James, and John, too. Matthias called out, "This must be the Comforter the Master spoke of," and he, too came under the spell.

Then everyone was praising the Lord aloud, and in different languages! Philip felt ecstatic. At last he was one with the Lord. Acutely aware of where he was and those around him, but at the same time he was oblivious to them. He focused only on the Lord.

Men on the street, attracted by the loud noise, came into the room. Peter quieted the room to welcome them and asked, "Will you join us?"

One man said, "Aren't you Galileans?"

Peter answered, "Most of us are, yes. Why do you ask?"

The man answered, "I am a Jew from Cyrene, and I heard God being praised in my own language."

Another said, "And I am from Mesopotamia. I heard someone using my language."

Another said, "I think they've had too much wine. They're all drunk. I heard someone speaking in Cretan."

Peter said, "It's only nine in the morning. We have not had too much wine. You are witnessing the fulfillment of prophecy. Stay and hear what I have to say." Led by the Holy Spirit, he quoted passages from the prophet

Joel. He told them about Jesus, who had come and was killed as prophecies foretold; that Jesus was the looked-for Anointed One and it was made known for certain when he arose from his tomb. Peter talked for an hour or more. As he talked others entered the room.

Finally, one of the newcomers asked, "I am overcome with grief that we have allowed this to happen. What can I do?"

Peter answered, "Repent and be baptized in the name of the Father, Son, and Holy Spirit, for the forgiveness of sins. Jesus' love extends to you and your children and all that he calls. You will receive his Comforter, the Holy Spirit."

All of those who had entered indicated that they wanted to repent and be baptized. Peter said, "We have only jars of water here. We need living water, a flowing stream. Let's go to the temple and use the pools there."

The apostles and disciples separated and went to the pools. The newcomers formed lines. As each forgiven man came up from the water, he walked away praising God in a language not before known to him.

At the end of the day the apostles and disciples returned to the upper room, tired but buoyed by the happenings. Peter happily said, "What a day, what a day. One to be well remembered." Then he asked, "How many do you think we added today?"

Matthew said, "There were 120 of us, and if each one baptized 30, we would have added 3,600."

John said, "I must have had at least forty."

Philip said, "I counted. I did thirty-five."

Another said, "I also counted, and I did twenty-eight."

Peter said, "Well, we can estimate a total of 4,000, then can't we? Praise God! I wonder what tomorrow will bring."

The next day was almost a repeat of the one before, and the day after, too. The apostles and disciples started preaching in the courts of the temple, since they were there for prayer anyway.

Sabbath was observed, for all the followers of Jesus were Jews. However, they also kept holy the first day of the week. They called it the Lord's Day, commemorating His resurrection from the grave. On this day the bread was broken in memory of Jesus' last meal with them, and when they drank their wine it was in memory of His death and shed blood. Scripture was read from the Prophets, finding nuggets foretelling of Jesus' ministry, death and resurrection.

The preaching and teaching went on seven days a week, and thousands of Jews were added daily to the followers of Jesus' teachings.

Near the end of a day about two weeks after Pentecost, Philip, Cleopas, and some of the other disciples had already returned to the upper room when the sound of someone running up the stairs caught their attention. The fear of being associated with Jesus had dissipated with the baptism of the Holy Spirit, and they had freely come and gone. With this sound, however, a sudden cessation of movement made each aware that they were still vulnerable to persecution.

"Peter and John have been arrested!" Andrew whispered as he burst into the room. Visions of three crosses on Calvary Hill came to Philip in the awesome silence that enveloped the room.

Chapter Sixteen

Two by two the apostles and disciples returned to the upper room. Some had not yet heard about the arrest of Peter and John; others had been witnesses.

"A lame man had just been healed," Matthew said as explanation. "The governing priests, the Sanhedrin, are fearful of our exploding growth."

"Should we disappear for awhile?" someone asked.

Silence, each waiting for another to speak in a leadership role. Jesus' brother James cleared his throat and softly said, "Jesus would--not want us to 'disappear.'" More silence. James took a deep breath and continued, "We should carry on as usual-- healing, preaching and teaching."

Matthew bit his upper lip, squinted his eyes, bit his lower lip. He said, "I agree. We have the Holy Spirit to guide our speech.

Aflame With The Spirit: Philip the Evangelist

We may be risking our lives, but we must remember--" He paused and then continued, "--we must remember that we promised to follow Jesus, even to death."

Silence returned. Everyone realized the serious consequences that may be theirs. Philip asked in a loud whisper, "Then we should go to the Temple tomorrow, as we have been doing?"

Almost in unison, the men answered in the same loud whisper, "Yes."

Matthew said aloud, "Yes, we must be prepared to carry on without Peter and John, or any other--mortal leader. We have the teachings of Jesus and are led by the Holy Spirit."

The sound of released tension exploded as each person renewed the commitment he had made to go into the world and make disciples.

Philip was now aware that he would be vulnerable to arrest and even death. Until this moment he had not faced the full impact of reality. To become a courier of the word, one must take responsibility of many things. *It's irony, yes, pure irony: here is something I know I'm cut out to do, and love every minute of. Yet, because of sharing this sacred*

Vada M Gipson

knowledge, there are those who would kill me through fear of losing their power to rule.

The evening was spent in prayer and meditation. Peter and John were in Philip's thoughts as he prayed and praised the Lord.

The next morning the apostles, disciples and many of the newly baptized followers were in the Temple. After praying, Philip said to Cleopas, "Shall we see if we can locate Peter and John?"

"That's a good idea. I've been thinking of them all night. Yes, let's do it."

A number of the others overheard, and someone said, "I want to go with you."

The group started out, when suddenly Cleopas called, "Look--look!" Coming toward them were Peter and John, walking freely toward the group.

"What a welcome surprise," Philip said. "What happened? Did they change--"

"Hold it. Hold it, Philip," Peter said, putting his arm around him. "Let's all go to the upper room. There's much to tell." Philip and Cleopas fell in behind Peter and John.

Once there, Peter said to those assembled, "Now, get comfortable. We have many things

Aflame With The Spirit: Philip the Evangelist

to discuss." Peter remained standing, looking at his fellow followers of Jesus.

"John and I have had a lot of time to think, and we have much to share with you. This event has revealed one of the things all of us will be facing, and we can expect more to come." He looked at each face to see if they were hearing him. He continued, "John and I feel that we must fortify you by telling of our experience. We have no doubt that our Lord Jesus was trying to prepare us for this eventuality, and we couldn't fathom His meaning."

Taking a deep breath, Peter said, "In His holy name, dear brothers, I ask that you hear me out. Miracles and wonders will be happening more and more, if we keep to the Way of Jesus. Whether to test our faith, or to give us a growing strength matters not. We have been privileged and honored to have been taught the mysteries of heaven and have been found worthy to receive the baptism of the Holy Spirit."

He hesitated, and continued slowly and deliberately, "These things were not wished on us. We--gladly--took the responsibility because we believed in serving our dear Lord Jesus, the Christ."

Looking at the men and women assembled, Peter saw all eyes were on him. A few had their mouths open, and all anxious to hear his next words.

"Ever since our beloved teacher was crucified a few months ago, strange things, as well as miracles, have happened all around us. We have been followed; we have been spied upon. Not by Rome, not even by Herod, but by our own race, Jews!"

Peter hesitated and appeared to be in deep thought. He grabbed his lips with his right hand and squeezed them lightly. Then he continued, "But for us, it has presented an annoying and possibly a more dangerous situation. We must expect and train ourselves to cope with these things."

The gathering started to squirm and several cleared their throats. Someone said, "Yes, yes, dear Peter, please go on. Tell us what happened to you and John."

"All right. Yesterday afternoon a series of strange events started as John and I were on our way to the Temple for prayer. We saw ahead of us a lame man, unable to walk. Two men had carried him and put him at the gate, the one called Beautiful, to beg of those coming and going. When he saw us looking

Aflame With The Spirit: Philip the Evangelist

at him he asked for alms. We explained that we carry no money but that we could give him something better. I asked him, 'Would you like to walk?' He answered, 'I have not walked during my whole life.' I repeated my question. He looked at us and I thought he was going to cry. I grabbed him by the right hand and said, 'In the name of our Lord Jesus Christ of Nazareth you will rise up and walk right now.' He started to shake his head. He looked at his legs then back up at me. I helped him to his feet. He took a couple of steps and started to yell, 'I can stand. I can stand!' I told him to take a lot of time until he became accustomed to it."

The room erupted with praises to God. Peter smiled, and said, "That is what happened yesterday. Everyone around us realized they had witnessed a miracle in the name of Jesus, and began to praise God. Well--" he hesitated before saying, "that was just the start of our strange events."

"What happened?" someone asked when Peter stopped for a deep breath.

"The healed man started to praise God, too, and followed us into the Temple. Everyone there recognized him as the lame beggar, and wanted to know what had happened. We explained how we called on the authority of Jesus, the Christ, to heal him, and if they would all turn to the Lord and repent of their sins and ask Him to forgive them He would do so."

John took up the story and said, "I had been noticing some Sadducees and priests standing in the background. When we were talking about the resurrection of the dead, they signaled the Temple Guards. They came over and told us we were under arrest. They took us to the prison, and we were there for the night."

Peter, taking it up again, said, "That's right, and at the hearing this morning, everyone in power was there--priests, scribes, elders, you name him, he was there. They brought us into the big room and made us stand in their midst. The High Priest stared at us for the longest time and finally asked, 'By what authority have you done this?'"

Jesus' brother James softly asked, "What was your response?"

John said, "You should have heard Peter!"

Peter interrupted, "Please, John--"

John, shaking his head, "No, Peter. I think they should know everything. We both felt the Holy Spirit upon us. Peter was magnificent!

Aflame With The Spirit: Philip the Evangelist

First he paid respect to the house and priests, then said, 'If you intend to convict us on the grounds of healing a sick man, and you are wondering where we get that authority, then let this be understood by you, and everyone in Judea, that we heal in the name of Jesus the Christ. The same man you crucified, who was raised from the dead. This is the authority with which we heal!' And Peter pointed to the healed man and said, 'And as living proof-- there stands the man who was healed.' He told them, 'We must do what is right in the sight of God. If it is different from what you desire then that is your problem. We must speak that which we have seen and heard.'"

Matthew asked, "What did they say when you told them that, Peter?"

Peter said, "When they saw these things they could not deny, they threatened to punish us if we continued with our ways. Then they released us."

John added, "We think they knew if they condemned us they might have an uprising that would bring the Roman soldiers."

James said, "We had come to the conclusion that we must be prepared to face arrest, or even death, but we must continue Jesus' work."

Peter said, "Let us pray and thank God for His power." Many prayers and praises were added.

Shortly thereafter Peter and John called the body of apostles and disciples together. Peter said, "We have a problem. Too many of us are going about preaching and healing, and the newcomers need further training."

James, Jesus' brother, said, "I don't feel comfortable in the role of a preacher, but I can organize classes for the converts, if you want me to."

Peter replied, "Fine, James. That's what we need, someone to take care of that part of our ministry." He looked at the other apostles sitting around him for approval and continued, "We'll give that job to you."

James said, "Those of you who wish to teach, let me know. If we keep the class size to twelve men, we will need most of you."

Philip, the son of a priest, was among those who raised their hands. He thought, *I am trained as a rabbi, I should have no problem.*

James continued, "We'll go into the homes. I think most of our new people live in this quarter of Jerusalem. They are accustomed

Aflame With The Spirit: Philip the Evangelist

to living communally. I don't see any need to change that, do you Peter?"

"No. We have lived that way since we started following Jesus. Matthew now holds our treasury. We can help feed the widows and orphans."

The body of apostles and disciples went to the Temple for early prayer. Afterward each of the designated teachers gathered twelve or so of the new people to form a class. He gave their names to James. The instructor went to a dwelling for the teaching. Philip's class met in the home of Ananias and his wife Sapphira.

About this time one of the newcomers by the name of Joseph Barnabas sold a field he owned. He brought the entire amount to Peter for the common treasury. Other converts followed Barnabas' example.

Philip asked Peter, "What has caused this outpouring?"

"Love, Philip. Love. The people want to share and are doing that which they can to make sure no one is hungry."

"Did you ask or make a rule?"

"No! What they do, they do freely. When Jesus' spirit touches them, they want to help others. He affects them just as He did us.

We must continue bearing witness to His resurrection."

Later Philip related to the members of his class the way some of the people were supporting the movement. He said, "I am telling you this just for your information. I am not suggesting that you do likewise, for that would be your decision."

One of the students asked, "If I were to sell a piece of property, would I have to turn over the entire amount of the sale to the treasury?"

"The land is yours to sell?" Philip asked.

"Let's say it is," was the answer.

"Then you can do whatever you want with it, rent it, farm it, sell it or let it lie fallow. Is that not right?"

"Yes."

Philip continued, "If you sold it, the money would be yours to do with as you pleased, the same as the property."

"Suppose I wanted to give only half to the treasury?"

Philip replied, "That would be your decision. However, if you sold it for a certain sum and told Peter you had sold it for half that amount, you would be lying, wouldn't you?"

"Yes."

Aflame With The Spirit: Philip the Evangelist

Philip remembered later, with relief, that Ananias was present at the time of the discussion.

Ananias and his wife Sapphira, subsequently, did go out and sell a bit of ground. They told Philip the amount they received, and that they intended turning it over to Peter. When Philip told Peter, he said, "It is good the people are so generous. We need funds to keep everyone fed."

Philip was with Ananias when he brought the money to Peter. Ananias said, "I have sold some property. Here are the proceeds from the sale for your treasury."

Peter asked Matthew to count it. When Matthew reported the amount, it was short by ten percent of the sum Philip had reported.

Peter asked Ananias, "You are giving the entire amount from the sale of your land?"

"Yes," Ananias answered.

Philip breathed deeply to confront Ananias with the higher figure that Ananias had told him. Just then Peter, incensed more than Philip had ever seen him, said in a loud voice, "You lie, Ananias. You have allowed Satan to enter your heart and have held back ten percent."

Ananias squirmed and started to protest when Peter continued, "When it was in your name, you could do anything you wanted to with it. Now you've sold it and tell me it was for an amount less than actually received. You didn't need to do that. If you planned on holding back some of it, that was entirely your own decision. But you must understand that in the work of the Holy Father and our dear departed Lord you must be truthful. In this situation, you are dealing with the Holy Spirit. In doing so, you must keep all of your channels clear to Him. You failed to do so. You deliberately set out to deceive that which has blessed us. It is the lie that causes the false pretense, and this exposes an unacceptable element in your heart. You didn't have to give any of it to the treasury. You've tried to deceive the Holy Spirit of God! Many before you have tried to do this. It can not be done!"

Ananias' hands grabbed his chest. Philip reached to support him, but he collapsed and slid to the floor.

Peter, who had been seated while Philip and Ananias had been standing, jumped up and stared at Ananias. The transition from life was taking place. He was lying with death's

Aflame With The Spirit: Philip the Evangelist

pallor coloring his skin, eyes sunken into his skull.

Philip softly said, "He's dead, Peter."

Peter's face showed a combination of shock and sadness. Philip's memory went back to the time Jesus changed Peter's name from Simon. Jesus told him, "Whoever you forgive will be forgiven in heaven, and whoever you condemn, will be condemned in heaven." Philip wondered if Peter knew he really possessed such power before this.

Peter shook his head in disbelief. As though to himself he muttered, "I should bring him back, but something won't let me. I felt death swoop him up like a great storm. What next?" Then looking at Philip he asked, "Where is his wife?"

"I don't know. I'll take a couple of men and go look for her."

Peter sat down, folding his left arm across his chest, placing his hand under the elbow of his right arm. He rubbed across his forehead with the fingers of his right hand, fingered his bushy eyebrows, then moving his hand to cup his weather-beaten face, his index finger across his mouth. Sitting up straight and taking a deep breath, Peter looked around the room and called, "Some of you young men, come and take care of this body and bury it."

Two hours later Philip and his two companions returned from their search. Peter looked up when they came through the doorway of the upper room. He had been getting up, pacing the room, and sitting down a dozen times. This time he got up, stretching his arms high and wide, and placed them on his hips. Looking at Philip, he inquired, "Nothing?"

"Nothing, Peter. We did meet the young men carrying Ananias' body out to be buried."

Peter stared at the floor and bit his upper lip in thought. Holding his hands behind his back he started to slowly pace the floor.

Philip sat down and reviewed the events of the day, searching for reason, or a message presented during this tragic episode. One thing stood out: it was not necessarily the fact that they had been watching fulfillment of prophecy the last few years, but something greater. Everything seems to be of a design-- or plan--on which future events depend. Philip felt awestruck when he thought of himself actually having a role, insignificant as it may be, in this great adventure. A privilege he had

Aflame With The Spirit: Philip the Evangelist

never dreamed of. He found himself again questioning his ability. *I still felt inadequate, especially at times such as today.*

Philip realized he was being drawn deeper into greater service to his beloved Master, and dear Peter. Philip thought, *how much I have learned just watching and listening to this great soul.* He knew how many tests Peter had been put through. He had seen tears in his eyes more than once. How hard it must be on him to be responsible for Ananias' death.

Philip's thoughts surfaced quickly when he became aware of Peter sitting beside him. Peter put his hand on Philip's shoulder and said, "I'm glad you joined our group. I believe you were led because you have always fit in so well." He paused a moment and stared at Philip.

Philip looked deep into his blue-gray eyes.

Finally, Peter continued, "I have found, besides the richness of memories of our Master, the greatest gift we've received is that of the Holy Spirit. He is always there--as long as we use Him properly. If ever we use His power against His will--I don't want to even think of what would happen to us. He makes Himself felt in many ways and we know He is the mind of God. Sometimes things may seem strange to us until something happens that we don't understand at the time, such as today, but afterward we can see where He has taken us and why."

Philip removed his gaze from Peter's face and slowly turned his head, looking into space thinking on Peter's words. Then he said slowly, "Yes—yes. Thank you, Peter. I needed your thoughts very much. You always say the right things at the right time."

Peter squeezed Philip's shoulder with a friendly grip and said, "Well, not always." Both men smiled.

Another hour passed.

Philip started to stand and stretch himself when Sapphira burst through the doorway. She had been running and was breathing quite heavily. "Have you--has Ananias been here?"

Peter slowly rose to his feet and stood erect, stretching his nearly six-foot frame. His eyes met hers and locked. Then she blinked and slowly dropped her stare to the floor.

Peter cleared his throat and asked slowly, "Yes, he's been here. Tell me, did you sell your field for this price?" And he named the amount Ananias had reported.

Aflame With The Spirit: Philip the Evangelist

She hesitated, raised her head and met his eyes, "Yes," she said, and tears started to flow down her face. "--for that price."

Footsteps were heard on the stairs. Peter clinched his jaws, inhaled slowly and said, "What you now hear are the men who have carried your dead husband to his grave. Because you were a part of the scheme to lie to the Holy Spirit, they shall now do the same for you."

The young men entered the room. Sapphira turned to look at them. She faced Peter again, raising her hand and started to say something. Her hand grabbed at her chest. She gave a little gasp and fell to the floor, dead. Everyone was amazed.

The fellows looked at Sapphira's body, then at Peter. He was watching them, and then turned to see how Philip was taking it. Philip saw her body on the floor, hardly believing the fast-moving events of the day. It had been but a short time since he'd talked about the sale of property in their home.

Peter said, "Well, my young brothers, the Holy Spirit has His own rules, sometimes quite severe. Therefore, let the happenings of this day remain as a strong lesson for life."

The young men wanted to know where they should bury her body.

"Well," Peter said, "I suppose it would be appropriate," he hesitated, raising his bushy eyebrows, then slowly lowering them into a deep frown, "if you buried her next to her husband."

Chapter Seventeen

Students of the disciples' classes were becoming preachers, healers and teachers. The sick and disabled from all around the area were brought into the city for healing. They lined the streets, and some were made well when Peter's shadow passed over them.

The scenes reminded Philip of Jesus' walks throughout Galilee. Jesus had told them, "These things you will do, and even greater." Philip wondered what greater things could they do than to offer the people Jesus' message of love and reconciliation with God, and healing for their bodies.

Some members of the Temple Guard and a large number of priests joined the movement. Classes for new converts continually had to be organized. Philip went to another commune as resident leaders took over the one in which Ananias and Sapphira had lived. James had a full-time job, keeping the records and forming new classes.

In the area where the apostles had been preaching one afternoon at the Temple, a commotion nearby distracted Philip from prayer. Temple Guards were arresting not only Peter and John, but also all of them. *No! Not again,* was his first thought. He wanted to follow as they were led away. What could be done to stop them? Realizing he was powerless, he turned to prayer, more earnestly than before. Feeling that Jesus was beside him, he told Him of his fears for the men, and asked protection by the Holy Spirit.

Before going to his residence he went to the upper room to notify those who may not have heard. Jesus' family was there: His mother, Mary, and His brothers James, Joseph, Simon, and Jude, as well as others. James said, "We will pray through the night, and we'll ask everyone else to do so."

Philip said, "I'll pass the word as I go to my dwelling."

At the nine o'clock the next morning, as Philip went up the Temple steps to pray, Peter and the Apostles were standing there--as if

Aflame With The Spirit: Philip the Evangelist

nothing had happened! *Was I seeing things?* Hurrying to them Philip said, "I saw the guards arrest you yesterday! Thank God, you are all free and unharmed." Other disciples were gathering around them.

His face beaming, Peter said, "Yes, we also praise God. He sent an angel in the night who opened the doors of our prison and led us out."

"Tell us more!" Philip urged.

John eagerly picked up the telling, "The angel said, 'Go and stand in the Temple and preach to the people the good news of God's love.'"

"So we were here when the guards came looking for us, this morning," Andrew added.

Philip asked, "Did they arrest you again?"

"In a way, yes. They made us go with them before the governing priests. But they were courteous about it," Andrew replied smiling and looking around at the other apostles.

"They were afraid of the people," John said.

"What happened?" Philip coaxed.

"The High Priest scolded us for continuing to preach Jesus crucified, dead, buried and resurrected after they had told us not to do so," Peter said.

"Then you should have heard Peter," John interjected. "He told them, 'We must obey God rather than you men. You hung Jesus on the cross, but the God of our fathers raised him from his tomb. He is now at the right hand of Jehovah as Prince and Savior to give repentance to Israel and remission of sins. We are witnesses to these things. His Holy Spirit has been sent to us and to those who obey him.'"

"I'm surprised they let you go, Peter. You must have been filled with the Pentecostal fire to be so brave," Philip said.

Peter replied, "They were upset, and for a moment I thought we would all be thrown into prison again, but one man, Gamaliel, a Pharisee, stood and spoke in our defense."

John continued, "He told them that if our movement is of God, there's nothing they could do to stop it. But if it is of men, it would die out, just like other persuasions have."

Philip said, "Well, you're here, so they must have let you go free."

"Yes, after warning us again not to preach, but after all we have seen and experienced, could you keep quiet, Philip?" Peter asked.

"No," Philip responded, "I'll probably be preaching or teaching with my dying breath."

Aflame With The Spirit: Philip the Evangelist

John said, "I feel honored to have suffered for preaching Jesus' crucifixion and resurrection. This movement will never die!"

The apostles' preaching and healing continued in the Temple, and new classes organized for the converts. Food was distributed from a central point in the Essene Quarter of Jerusalem.

After a few weeks, one evening a contingent of men came to Peter in the upper room. The spokesman said, "Peter, even though we speak only Greek, we are Jews. Our widows are being overlooked in the daily ration of food. Something has to be done about it."

Peter said, "I'm sorry to hear it, and you're right, we must correct the problem."

After the men had gone, Peter called the apostles together to discuss a solution. Thereafter, notice was sent to the original followers of Jesus to come together.

At the assembly, Peter explained the situation and said to them, "We apostles don't have time to do everything. Our most important task is to pray, preach and heal. So, we want you to select seven Greek-speaking men from among you whose job it will be to see that everyone receives a fair share of the food."

Everyone was in agreement that this sounded like a good plan. Among those chosen were Stephen, a spirit-filled disciple, and Philip. He thought: *I am always surprised at the turn of events. I suppose I'll never get accustomed to the ways Jesus will use me.*

The seven were brought to the front of the assemblage. Peter prayed, "Our Father in heaven, precious is your name. We pray your granting special insights to these men that they may fairly distribute from your bounty. In Jesus' name I pray. Amen." Then he dipped his thumb in a cup of oil and as he touched the forehead of each said, "God bless you."

After the other Disciples had returned to their dwellings, the seven made plans as to how they were going to fulfill their commission. All but Stephen had classes at various stages of training. He had just finished his and was ready to move on, turning that household leadership over to a resident. So he was selected to be the one in charge, at least for the time being. As the others became available they would take their turn. When all were free of teaching duties, the responsibility

Aflame With The Spirit: Philip the Evangelist

would rotate so they, too, could pray, preach and heal.

Philip's class ended in two weeks, and he moved back to the upper room where Stephen had again taken up residence. Philip helped him a few days to learn the system Stephen had worked out.

Stephen was anxious to get back to preaching. Not only did he go out on the streets, but taught in the Greek-speaking synagogues within the city of Jerusalem.

Philip's routine became one of going to the food storage house, and carefully supervising helpers to fairly distribute the daily ration of food. Rather than have his assistants take the food to the communes, a representative of each dwelling came to the storage house and was given the allotment for the number of people in their home. The Greek-speaking Jews, Hellenists, were satisfied with this arrangement.

In time, another of the chosen seven relieved Philip, and he, too, could once more go out on the streets to preach and heal. He and Stephen would go together to the Temple for the third-hour prayer, and then separate.

The first Passover after Jesus' death and resurrection was approaching, and the city was once again filling with pilgrims. One morning, as Philip was in the open court of the Temple preaching, he saw the guards escorting Stephen inside. *Has he been arrested?* He excused himself from his listeners, and followed after Stephen.

As Stephen's group approached the inner court where the Sanhedrin met, two Temple guards met Philip and the group with him. "You can go no farther," one guard said.

Philip looked directly at the man and recognized him as one who recently accepted Jesus as the Messiah. Speaking softly, Philip asked, "What are they going to do with him?"

"He'll be questioned is all. Some of the Hellenists in the synagogues where he has been preaching have objected to what he is saying, and complained to the Chief Priest. You know they do not have the authority to put him to death."

"But they can imprison him, as they did Peter and John!"

"Yes, but after their last attempt at arresting them, I think the apostles are safe. They'll pick on leaders who are not so well known, like Stephen--and you!"

Aflame With The Spirit: Philip the Evangelist

"Me?" Philip asked in astonishment. *What an honor. To be considered a leader close enough to Jesus to be arrested.*

"Yes, you!" He slowly added, "A new man, Saul of Tarsas, has come back to Jerusalem. He is stirring up the priests to do away with leaders of this movement."

Philip stared at the guard trying to read his expression, "Thank you for that information." After a moment of hesitation, he continued, "What can I do to help Stephen?"

"Pray. He will have to defend himself by his wits, but he's full of the Holy Spirit and a good speaker. I know. I've listened to him many times."

"I agree that he preaches a lucid message. He'll either convert them, or make them so angry that they'll throw him in prison."

A little smile tickled the guard's face. The other guard was beginning to fidget at the long conversation with Philip. In a loud voice Philip said to the group with him, "Come on folks, we need to be in prayer for Stephen. Go, and pass the word."

Philip went to the upper room to inform those who were there. Peter's wife had arrived from Capernaum, as had the wives and children of several of the other apostles and

Jesus' brothers. Philip greeted and welcomed them to Jerusalem.

To James, he told of Stephen's arrest and the need for prayer in his behalf. Then he added, "I feel an urgent push to go back to the Temple. I must keep watch."

"All right, Philip. I'll pray for you, too."

Philip retraced his steps to the Temple. In the Court of the Gentiles, he was drawn to the far side, the one that faced Kidron Valley and Mount of Olives.

Just then a crowd of men came out of the Court of the Priests dragging Stephen! The priests followed. Philip could see no way of going to Stephen's aid. Stephen was shouting, "Are you going to kill me, too? Just like you've killed every messenger from God? When will you ever learn that God wants to be reconciled with you? You never give him a chance!"

The men pulled Stephen to the gate through the wall. Philip ran to see where they were taking him. Just as he went through the gate, he saw Stephen thrown bodily into the ravine. The men began picking up large stones and throwing them at Stephen. They are stoning him to death!

Aflame With The Spirit: Philip the Evangelist

"I see Jesus! He's at the right hand of God," Stephen yelled. *He sounds at peace. How can he be?*

Then Philip heard, "Gracious Lord Jesus, take my spirit. Forgive these men, they know not what they do."

Philip ran to the edge. He saw that Stephen had knelt, and put his head forward so a stone could hit it squarely. As Philip watched, Stephen was struck, went limp, and died.

A loud cry arose from the men. One near Philip said, "That should put a stop to his heresy." Philip noticed that the priests, themselves, did not participate in the stoning, but stood back observing, such as he had done.

Among the observers was one to whom they seemed to be catering favors. Short of stature, he had a hooked nose, typical of Jewish men, and a baldhead with heavy eyebrows nearly meeting at the center of his forehead. *Is he the man the guard told me about? Did he say Saul of Tarsas?*

Chapter Eighteen

"Peter!" Philip called as he entered the upper room. "We must talk. Something dreadful is happening."

"Is happening? Something dreadful?" Peter repeated questioningly.

"Oh, yes. Is happening and we must do something to stop it, and soon."

"Is it about Saul?" Peter asked.

"Then you know?"

"Yes. I have received several reports of him and his supporters rushing into homes of believers of The Way, beating and terrorizing them."

Cleopas, coming to stand beside Philip, began waving his arms wildly, said "People are leaving Jerusalem, going back to where they came from. We're losing our following."

When Peter didn't respond, Jesus' brother, James, who was seated nearby, softly said, "It

Aflame With The Spirit: Philip the Evangelist

may be that--we're not losing it so much as--as this is a way to--to grow."

Peter, turning to James, said, "I'm a simple man. Just what are you saying?"

James stood, looking out across the room--and beyond--placing his hand on his graying bearded chin. Taking a few steps, he turned and slowly walked toward Peter as though giving thought as to how to answer. Stopping in front of him he started to speak slowly, "I, like all of you, have been expecting our Lord to return at any time. Now, I think we should prepare ourselves for His return eventually, but not immediately."

Peter said, "Oh? Well, go on."

James took a few steps as if he had a new concept that had not been thought through, spoke as he paced, "If our people go back home and--and take their belief with them, carry on that which we have been doing here--" The room was silent as he paused longer than usual during his hesitant speech, continued, "Didn't Jesus say something about the kingdom of God being like yeast?"

"James!" yelled Peter, jumping to his feet, his countenance lit up as he almost shouted, "Of course! Yes! I understand. Yes!" Clapping his hands together. "Good for you, James, here in our midst where there is nothing but bullies and cruelty at work we see--"

Absolute silence hung over the room. Peter stared at the floor, took in a deep breath and said softly and slowly, "Yes--" Then louder, "Yes! What a plan of action! There's more to serving our Lord than we thought. This persecution is causing great alarm. It is now that we are aroused into greater action. Our emotions are high--Yes, James, that's the answer. Jesus said, 'Go to all nations and make disciples.'" Chuckling to himself, he added, "Won't Saul be surprised when he learns that he was used by God to spur us into going beyond Jerusalem!"

Everyone was watching Peter and his every move. He continued, "This gives all of us something to really pray about--to have the Holy Spirit guide us into a singular vein for the glory of God and our dearly beloved Master."

Each person was smiling as silence descended on the group that was made up of the apostles, Jesus' brothers, the remainder of the chosen seven known as Elders, and other disciples. The atmosphere was filled with excitement. It was as if each one had received a new challenge, a special assignment to be carried out in his own way.

Philip felt the nearness of the Master, as if He were just waiting for them to formulate a plan of action. Philip was making his own decision about how he was going to respond.

"Who among us will go?" someone asked.

Another, "Who will stay? We'll have to keep a home synagogue to remain organized."

James said, "We're Jews. I think Jerusalem should remain our central church." After a moment's hesitation, he continued, "If you like, I'll continue on as I have been doing, keeping the records--right here in Jerusalem."

John said, "Thank you, James. You are well suited for that job. And it would free the disciples to pick a country and carry on that which we've started here." Turning to address Peter, he continued, "As for us apostles, I think we should stay here as long as possible."

Excitement due to the prospect of being sent out once again to preach, teach and heal caused everyone to talk at once. "Quiet!" yelled Peter. "Let's go to prayer, and give ourselves a little time to get used to this idea. We'll come together again tomorrow after third-hour prayer."

The next morning everyone assembled in the great synagogue where the baptism of the Holy Spirit took place. The apostles occupied the seats on the dais, facing the room full of men and women. Peter prayed for the presence of the Holy Spirit to guide his words, and then said, "Brothers and sisters in Jesus, the Christ: As followers of The Way, we have come to a fork in the road. Many of the people are being persecuted for their beliefs, and others are leaving Jerusalem to save themselves from the same treatment."

An affirmation came from the body of listeners.

Peter continued, "We who were closest to Jesus want to remain here, and be a central church. After all, we are Jews. I agree completely with James and John. Where better than Jerusalem to have our headquarters?"

Voices of agreement were heard from around the hall.

"One of the first things Jesus said after his resurrection was, 'As the Father has sent me, I send you.' Now is the time for the sending. He trained us well...twice he sent us two by two out into villages without purse or extra clothing. Since this will be for an indefinite period of time, we believe those who go

Aflame With The Spirit: Philip the Evangelist

should take whatever they can carry. Now, plan well and study the situation as you go. Every move you make will be watched, so pray constantly for guidance by the Holy Spirit."

A voice from the room asked, "Will you assign us destinations, as was done before?"

Peter looked at the other apostles who shrugged as if they didn't have an answer. Then he answered, "You can pick the area, but James will keep a record so you won't be running into each other. Remember, we are to preach to Jews only. Follow the pattern established, go to the synagogue and start your ministry with the people there."

Philip asked, "May I go back to Caesarea? I made many friends there."

Peter again visually consulted the other apostles and found no objection. He said, "Your friends are Jews?"

"Most of them are. Caesarea is a crossroad of the world, and people from all over are there. What happens if someone who isn't a Jew comes to hear and is converted?"

Peter received a negative indication from his fellow apostles. He said, "It would be as the proselyte. He would have to accept the badge of our religion."

"Do you mean circumcision?" Philip asked.

"Yes," Peter replied.

A murmur from the room of men was heard.

Another Elder asked, "What about communal living--sharing food, money and living space?"

Several "Yes, what about it?" were heard from those in the hall.

Peter looked at him for a long moment. Then he said, "It hasn't worked too well here among people who weren't used to it, has it?"

Philip thought of the grievance of the Greeks for their widows and the deaths of Ananias and Sapphira.

"No," was answered back from the listeners.

Peter looked at his fellow apostles to see if there was anything to be said on the subject. Some were shaking their heads. Peter said, "Don't force it. You will continue Jesus' teachings of sharing that which we have with those in need. If communal living comes about naturally, you'll know it's right with the Holy Spirit."

Philip felt relieved that point had been cleared up.

Aflame With The Spirit: Philip the Evangelist

Philip asked Cleopas to be his partner on the mission to Caesarea. They departed Jerusalem early the following morning, heading north through Bethel into the country of Samaria. Philip had never been that route before.

Approaching Jacob's well late in the afternoon of the second day, Cleopas told Philip of being there with Jesus on one of his trips. Jesus had waited at the well while the disciples had gone into the town to buy some food. When they returned they found Jesus talking to a Samaritan woman! She ran off toward town calling, "The Messiah has come! He's at the well." Cleopas ended his story with, "We spent two days in Sychar, and many of those Samaritans became believers."

"If Jesus talked to Samaritans, and accepted their hospitality for two days, why did he tell us to avoid them?" Philip asked.

"It was before this incident at the well when he sent us out with those instructions. Later Jesus told us, 'I have other sheep in my fold.' I've often wondered if he meant Samaritans or Gentiles as a whole."

Taking a few slow paces in silence, Philip stopped and half turned. He said, "Well, let's be open to the Holy Spirit. If we have the opportunity, we'll tell our good news to anybody who will listen. Do you agree?"

"I agree. Ah! Here it is. How about a drink from the well that your forefather Jacob dug?"

After swallowing a few refreshing sips of the cold water and sitting on the rock wall built around the well, Philip said, "I am thrilled to be here. So much of our people's history took place in this area--and I never expected to be here in person!"

"Yes," Cleopas replied. Pointing, he said, "Over there are Mt. Gerizim and Mount Ebal where Moses had representatives of six tribes of Jacob go up each mountain and he read the covenant of the blessings and cursings of the Law."

"Let me guess. The one with the trees is Gerizim, the one of the blessings, right?"

"Right! The barren one is Ebal, where the 'amens' of the cursings were said. And Joshua built the altar at Shechem after he had won this area in battle. We'll see it as we go through town."

Philip responded, "Wasn't it at Shechem where Abraham received the word from God that this was the Promised Land?"

"Yes."

"I can understand why the Samaritans take pride in their heritage--it is the same as ours! Mount Gerizim was more holy than Jerusalem in those days."

"It was those individuals who adopted the ways and religion of the conquered race and intermarried with them while the Jews were in captivity that caused the problem between us," Cleopas explained. "That's their temple," he added, pointing at a beautiful building on Mt. Gerizim.

Philip stood and stretched his body, reaching his hands high. He said, "Well, if we want to get to Samaria City before dark, we had better move on."

Chapter Nineteen

Dusk found them near Sebaste, the new name Herod the Great had given Samaria City. Inasmuch as it was built on a hilltop, Philip and Cleopas decided to stay the night near the road bound for Caesarea. They approached a house set back from the road. A dog in the yard started barking to alert the homeowner of their arrival.

"Shalom!" Philip called. "We come in peace."

A man came out the courtyard door, staring at Philip and Cleopas.

"We are travelers on our way to Caesarea. Could we accept your hospitality to spend the night here?" Philip asked.

The man stepped inside the door to his courtyard bringing out a lighted torch to see them better. Philip thought: *he looks familiar-- where have I seen him?*

Aflame With The Spirit: Philip the Evangelist

The man jabbed his light in Philip's face and stared at him, then at Cleopas. He turned back to Philip, and asked, "Where's Judas?"

Relaxing from a tension of which he was unaware and a smile twitching at the corners of his mouth, Philip knew where he had seen him before. "It's a long story. Judas is dead."

"Dead?" He looked hard at Philip. "Well, come on in. I have to hear this long story." He turned to lead the way into the courtyard of his home. Waiting inside were a woman and three children, ranging in age from about twelve to three years. To the woman he said, "Bring some food for these sojourners." To the men he said, "Make yourselves comfortable. My wife will bring you some refreshment." Handing Philip a towel, he said, "You may wash at the basin over there."

Philip said, "Thank you." Taking the few steps to the table the basin was on, he continued, "I didn't expect to see you again. May I ask your name?"

"Shemer."

"Ah, that's right--Shemer of Samaria City, Judas' robber friend." As he washed his hands and dried them he said, "My name is Philip. I'm from Julias, and--" handing the towel to Cleopas, "--this is my friend Cleopas of Emmaus."

Shemer nodded to Cleopas, and he in turn bowed and said, "Thank you for your gracious hospitality."

After Cleopas had washed his hands and dried them the two men sat beside the table on mats provided them by the children. The youngsters gathered around their father, who sat facing the men. Their faces showed curiosity of these strangers.

"After you pray tell me about Judas. He wasn't with me long, but I took a liking to him."

While the men ate, they started relating the story of Judas' betrayal and Jesus' crucifixion. The meal was long over and the children bedded down for the night when Philip and Cleopas told of Judas' suicide.

"So he killed himself! I didn't think he had the courage to do such a thing! He must have been really disappointed in the man." Shemer thought a minute, studying his folded hands, looked up and said, "This 'Jesus' person, was he from Nazareth, the one Judas told me to remember--that he was the Messiah?"

Aflame With The Spirit: Philip the Evangelist

Philip and Cleopas answered together, "Yes." Then Philip continued, "Yes, Jesus of Nazareth IS the Messiah."

A frown-crease in Shemer's brow deepened. "I thought you said he died on the cross. How can you say he IS the Messiah?" Shemer asked, incredulously.

A broad smile came to both faces of the men. Philip said, "Because He arose from the grave, and appeared to us. We saw Him, talked with Him, ate with Him, and so did many others!"

"No! Come on, now. You don't expect me to believe such a fantasy, do you?" Shemer asked.

Cleopas said, "Shemer, you are a Samaritan, aren't you?"

Sitting up straight, as though he took pride in his lineage, said, "Yes."

Cleopas continued, "Then you believe in Abraham, Jacob, and Moses, our common forefathers?"

Again Shemer said, "Yes."

"You know the scriptures prophesied the coming of a Savior, don't you?"

"Indeed I do. I was raised, and I'm bringing up my sons with teachings from the Torah."

Deliberately, Cleopas said, "Jesus of Nazareth during His life, His death, and His resurrection, fulfilled all the prophecies!"

Opening his mouth, raising his bushy eyebrows, then slowly lowering them, looking into each of their faces, Shemer said, "Really?"

"Really." Cleopas and Philip affirmed together.

"Please, I want to hear more. I want to hear all about this."

Far into the night Shemer, his wife sitting back in the shadows, listened to Philip and Cleopas, asking a question now and then. They found him to be no different than their friends who were Jews.

Along toward morning, Shemer said, "What must we do to become followers of your Way, and be reconciled to God through Jesus?"

Philip said, "Do you repent of all your wrong-doings against God and man?"

Shemer hesitated, "Yes, I know robbery is breaking one of Moses' commandments, and I wouldn't have done it if I had another way to feed my family, but I am truly sorry for that which I have done, and I hope I won't have to do it again!"

Aflame With The Spirit: Philip the Evangelist

"As a follower of the Way, your needs will be taken care of. Of course, to make it happen, you have to provide the Holy Spirit with your service. I have one more question: do you accept Jesus as the Messiah?"

Shemer answered, "I do." Turning to his wife, he asked, "What about you, Dinah?"

From the quietness of the edge of the courtyard came a soft, "Yes. I do, too."

Philip asked, "Do you have a swimming hole around here that has running water where we can baptize you?"

"Yes, we have a spring that supplies the water for the city through aqueducts and cisterns. It's a little way from here, but we can go there tomorrow."

"All right." Philip rose to a standing position, stretched, and looked at Cleopas who had a broad smile and was starting to stand, too. Philip said, "I feel like singing a psalm of praise." Turning to Dinah asked, "Will you join us?" By now Shemer also was standing.

She answered as she approached the men, "I don't sing very well, but I'll try."

Shemer laughed and said as he reached for Dinah's hand to hold, "Imagine--me! An old robber, singing a psalm of praise!"

Cleopas said, "When you come in contact with Jesus you find yourself wanting to do a lot of things that used to be contrary to your nature."

It took a moment to orient himself the next morning when Philip awakened. He and Cleopas had spent the remainder of the night in the courtyard. The sun was high. He usually arose at dawn. Having walked for two days and talking with Shemer far into the night had made him sleep later than usual. Cleopas was still breathing deeply.

Then Philip heard giggles coming from the cooking area, followed by a "Sh-sh." He was reminded of the many nights, when he was still paralyzed, he slept in the courtyard at his home in Julias and of his own daughters. He realized that he missed them more than he had thought he did. *Well, as soon as I am established in Caesarea, I will send for them as I have promised.*

Philip turned over to look into the kitchen where the children were helping themselves to some breakfast. They saw him watching them and waved to him. He winked back to acknowledge their greeting.

Aflame With The Spirit: Philip the Evangelist

Just then Cleopas opened his eyes. He saw that Philip was awake, but still on his sleeping pallet, then he saw the children.

They waved to him. He said, "Good morning!"

Giggles broke out from the children. They didn't have to keep quiet any longer.

Shemer and Dinah came down the stairs into the courtyard. Shemer said, "We all overslept this morning, didn't we?"

Philip and Cleopas rose up off their pallets. Philip said, "I slept soundly. How about you?"

Shemer said, "We were so uplifted that we couldn't fall asleep. But we feel refreshed this morning and are looking forward to being baptized."

"All right. You lead the way, and we'll do the rest. But first we need to go to prayer."

Shemer said, "Of course."

After prayers, Shemer said, "The spring is in the hillside, about a mile on the far side of Sebaste, but we may use the pool in the bathhouse in town, if that's all right. It has water running in and out all the time."

Philip said, "That will be just perfect. It will give us a chance to see the city."

On the climb up the hill on which Sebaste was built, Shemer hailed friends and neighbors along the way, "We're going to be baptized into Jesus of Nazareth. Come on along." The party stopped when they reached the center of town where the bathhouse was located. Philip and Cleopas turned and were surprised to see the number of people who had followed them. Someone said, "Who is this Jesus of Nazareth?" Someone else said, "I've heard of him from friends in Sychar." Another said, "Tell us about him."

Philip and Cleopas looked at one another. This was too good to be true. Here was a ready-made audience, asking to hear the news they were anxious to share! Philip turned to Shemer and asked, "Are we allowed to talk here?"

"As long as we remain peaceful, we can meet anywhere. The Romans don't like too much agitation that would lead to trying to overthrow them."

"Followers of Jesus' Way are lovers of peace," Philip replied. Turning to the people who had followed, Philip said, "We'll be happy to share our good news of Jesus, who is the Messiah." And he and Cleopas reviewed the passages in the Torah and the Prophet Jeremiah where God had promised to send a redeemer.

Aflame With The Spirit: Philip the Evangelist

Passers-by, hearing the speakers, stopped to listen. The crowd grew. Philip and Cleopas broke their teaching at the third and sixth hours for prayer. The people joined in. The ninth hour was approaching when someone from the crowd said, "Can I be baptized, too?"

Philip replied, "Do you repent of your transgressions?"

A loud, "Yes," came from the crowd. Philip visibly jumped at the sound, and he and Cleopas smiled broadly.

Then he asked, "Do you accept Jesus of Nazareth as the Messiah?"

Again the resounding, "Yes," came from the assemblage of people.

"We'll be happy to baptize you in the name of Jesus, right here in these bathing pools. Make lines. Cleopas will take one line in this pool, and I'll go over there."

Someone said, "Will you be here tomorrow? I have family and friends that I would like to hear you."

Philip and Cleopas looked at each other. Shemer said, "You're welcome to stay with me as long as you wish."

Philip, looking at the questioner, said, "Yes. We'll be here tomorrow. Tell all your friends and neighbors."

So began an unforeseen and unexpected ministry of preaching, teaching and healing to the Samaritans.

As the days went by the numbers increased, just as had happened before in Caesarea and Jerusalem.

Philip was aware of one distinguished-looking man who seemed to be a leader among the citizens of the city. He was first among those who accepted Jesus as the Christ and asked to be baptized. Thereafter, he was at Philip's side wherever he went in the city. Simon was his name.

When asked, Shemer told Philip, "Simon is a well-known magician here in Sebaste. People believe he has the power of God. He's impressed with the healings you two are doing. I've seen him do some of his tricks, and he is good, but he hasn't cured anyone yet. Perhaps he's accompanying you everywhere so he can learn your magic."

Philip said, "But I have no magic. I have the name of Jesus, the Messiah."

Shemer answered, "I know that and you know it, but does Simon?"

Aflame With The Spirit: Philip the Evangelist

After a few days, Cleopas started a home study group as had been done in Jerusalem, and more people were being baptized.

But no one was receiving the baptism of the Holy Spirit. Philip and Cleopas were talking about this oddity when Philip said, "I would like Peter to know what's happening here."

Cleopas said, "If you will appoint someone to teach my class, I'll go and give him the report."

"All right. That will be great," Philip replied.

Cleopas left the following morning.

Peter and John were with him five days later when he returned. They were at Shemer's when Philip came from preaching in Sebaste. Embraces were exchanged. Philip was happy the two leaders from Jerusalem felt this ministry in Samaria important enough to warrant the presence of both.

Peter said, "Cleopas has been telling us about the works of the Holy Spirit here, and I want to hear more from you Philip, but first," reaching into his pouch and bringing out a small scroll, "here's a letter from your family."

Philip looked at the scroll, and reached for it with trepidation. Did it contain bad news?

Leaving the men talking to Shemer, Philip took the scroll to a secluded niche outside the courtyard to read it in privacy.

After reading it through, Philip felt grateful that the letter contained mostly local happenings concerning his family and friends. He read it again before rolling it up. He thought: *I miss them. I will write and tell them all is well.* He returned to the courtyard to visit with Peter and John.

"Thank you, Peter. It was a nice letter from my family. My father-in-law included the news about the death of our tetrarch, and his kingdom being given to the Province of Syria. Of all of Herod's children, he was the best. His rule has been peaceful. Rome is still in control, though, and no one knows what it will mean to be part of Syria."

Peter said, "Yes, I'd heard about that. We'll just have to wait and see, I suppose. Now, let me tell you how excited we are in Jerusalem by the news Cleopas brought us about the work here in Samaria City. We didn't expect to have a response from them, you know."

Philip looked at Shemer to see his reaction. Shemer picked up Philip's concern and laughed. "You're a man I can identify with,

Aflame With The Spirit: Philip the Evangelist

Peter. I often say the first thing that comes to me, and sometimes I get into trouble."

Peter at first looked perplexed, and then laughed, "I'm sorry, Shemer. I just felt that you are one of us so much that I forgot you are one of those--Samaritans."

"I am one of you, now, but I am still a Samaritan, just like you will always be a Jew. But we both have chosen to follow Jesus and his teachings, so that makes us brothers," Shemer responded.

Peter walked to where Shemer was standing and embraced him and said, "Brother."

John said, "Cleopas tells us that no one has received the baptism of the Holy Spirit. Can you explain why?"

Philip said, "No. We've done everything just as we did in Jerusalem. At least we tried to."

Peter said, "Let's pray about it tonight, and tomorrow we'll go with you into the city. I may even preach to the people, myself."

Philip looked into Peter's blue-gray eyes. "That would be wonderful."

The next morning found Peter, John, Philip and Cleopas in the center of Sebaste, and the usual crowd starting to gather when Philip began preaching. Then it came time for them to be baptized. Peter and John observed closely. No one received the Holy Spirit, so Peter asked them to come to him and John. Peter prayed and the two of them laid their hands on the individuals, and they received the Holy Spirit.

Simon the magician was in the forepart of the observers. He saw the happy glow of serenity descend on those receiving the Holy Spirit, some singing, others speaking in foreign languages. He said to Peter, "Will you teach me how to do that? I have money that I can pay you."

Peter angrily responded, "Money can't buy it, and your asking shows that your heart is not right with God."

A blank look came on the magician's face, and he stared at Peter.

Peter commanded, "Repent of this wickedness and ask God's forgiveness."

Simon looked down, his shoulders sagging. "I'm sorry," he softly said. "Will you pray for me?"

Peter continued to stare at the man, as though he was trying to read his heart. Then he said, "All right, we'll pray for you." Peter

Aflame With The Spirit: Philip the Evangelist

offered a prayer on Simon's behalf, laid his hands on him and Simon, too, received the baptism of the Holy Spirit.

Philip and Cleopas thereafter laid hands on the people after baptism, and they received the Holy Spirit.

Peter and John remained in Sebaste for a week, observing the Sabbath and the Lord's Day with their new friends before returning to Jerusalem.

When parting, Philip said, "I am beginning to wonder if the Lord really wants me to go to Ceasarea."

Peter replied, "You're a good man, Philip, keeping yourself open to the guidance of the Holy Spirit. If Ceasarea is to be your mission, you will go there. And now, Philip, we must leave both of you to continue your work. John has his calling, and I must find a place for my family to live."

Peter placed his hands on Philip's upper arms, smiled at him, and said, "Shalom, Philip."

Philip smiled back at this giant soul in front of him and said softly, "And shalom to you, Peter."

Chapter Twenty

A week later, after a long day of teaching, preaching, and healing, Philip and Cleopas retired early and slept soundly into the night.
"Philip."
Suddenly Philip was awake. He opened his eyes, slowly orienting himself. The form of Cleopas was on his mat, snoring softly. Philip looked around for a source of the voice. He was certain he had heard some one call his name. Starlight revealed no one else in Shemer's courtyard. *I must have been dreaming.* He closed his eyes to go back to sleep.

As he was drifting off, he definitely heard it again, "Philip." Opening his eyes once more he saw a shimmering light in the dark shadows. It took the form of a man. He didn't look like Jesus. Sitting up, Philip said softly, "Is that you, Lord?"

Aflame With The Spirit: Philip the Evangelist

"No. I am His messenger. You are to rise and go south."

"South? Caesarea is north. That's where we were going."

"Yes, south. Go back to Jerusalem and take the road to Gaza in the desert."

"Now?" Philip asked incredulously.

"Yes, now. I will guide you. Fear not."

"To Gaza in the desert," Philip repeated dazedly.

The form disappeared.

Philip reached over and touched Cleopas, who had slept undisturbed through the encounter with the angel. He called softly, "Cleopas."

Cleopas turned over and Philip, again, softly said his name. Cleopas opened his eyes and looked directly into Philip's. "What is it?" he sleepily asked.

"You'll find it hard to believe, but an angel of the Lord was just here."

Now fully awake, Cleopas asked, "An angel?"

"Yes, and he told me to get up right now and go back to Jerusalem, and take the road to Gaza in the desert. Have you ever been there?"

"An angel!" Cleopas was still attempting to comprehend. "What did you say he wanted?"

Philip repeated his instructions adding, "You must remain here to shepherd this new congregation." Eyeing Cleopas to make sure he was fully awake, Philip said, "Do you understand what I am saying?"

"Yes--I think so."

Philip asked him again if he had been to Gaza in the desert.

"Yes. It's on a main trade route to Egypt. So many battles have been fought there that not much is left. The new Gaza is closer to the great sea."

"Can you tell me how to go out of Jerusalem?"

"Take the road to Bethlehem. People on the road will help you."

Philip arose from the mat, washed his face and hands in the water basin, and came back to where Cleopas lay. "Tell Shemer and Dinah goodbye for me, and thank them for their hospitality."

Cleopas sat up on his mat. "Will you come back here?" he asked.

"I just don't know where the Holy Spirit will lead me. I'll try to let you know. You're a good traveling companion, and an excellent

Aflame With The Spirit: Philip the Evangelist

leader for Sebaste. May God be with you, Cleopas."

"And also with you, my friend."

Philip felt an urgency to keep walking. It was more than forty miles from Sebaste to Jerusalem, but he had an early start. Wanting to be in the upper room for the night, he allowed his pace to slow, but very little, during the heat of the afternoon. Compared with the Jordan River Valley, it wasn't bad at all. It was evening when he arrived at the house.

The owner greeted him warmly as did his brother, the healed blind man. Quietly going up the stairs, his heart started beating harder as he thought of the news he had to tell his friends. He knocked on the locked door of the upper room.

"Who is it?" asked a voice from within.

"Philip, returned from Sebaste."

The door was unlocked and opened. "Welcome back, Philip! This is a happy surprise. Are you alone?" It was James, Jesus' brother, reaching to embrace him.

"Yes. Cleopas remains in Sebaste," Philip said, stepping inside the room. No one else was there. "Where's Peter?"

"Peter has found a place to live with his wife and family. And John and James and Mother are at Bethany with Lazarus." Hesitating a moment, he continued, "We thought it wise to separate--not all be at the same place at the same time."

"Saul is still giving trouble?" asked Philip as he made his way to where the food was kept.

"Yes. The idea of our people leaving Jerusalem rather than be harassed by him and his ruffians seems to be a good one. They're not giving up their belief in Jesus as the Christ. We've heard from some of them. They're starting study groups in their home towns."

Fixing himself some cheese and bread, Philip said, "That's good news. Isn't it beautiful, when you think about God's plan and how it is working out?"

"I agree. We've heard from people in the Temple that Saul has been given a letter to carry on his dirty work in Damascus. So we here in Jerusalem will be free of him for awhile, but I pity followers of The Way when he gets there!"

Aflame With The Spirit: Philip the Evangelist

Philip stopped eating, looked hard at James and finally asked, "Is there any way to warn them?"

Pausing before answering, James said, "Yes, I believe there is a way." Hesitating, James slowly said, "Ananias went to Damascus. We need to send him a letter."

"Do you know of anyone going, faster than walking?" Philip asked.

James replied, "We have brothers within the palace. They may be able to deliver a letter for us quickly." Looking at Philip with a twinkle in his eye asked, "Would you like to write it?"

"Yes, I'll be glad to."

"Fine. I write, and don't mind keeping records, but letters don't come easy for me," James replied.

So Philip wrote the letter to Ananias in Damascus, telling him of the treatment followers of The Way could expect from Saul when he arrived.

James said, "I'll take this to the palace first thing tomorrow morning, and try to get it included in the packet going to Damascus." Taking a deep breath he asked, "How are things in Sebaste?"

Philip shared with him all the good news from Old Samaria City, ending with his fantastic encounter with the angel, and "That's what has brought me here, tonight."

"What do you think is at Old Gaza that God wants you to go there? From what I understand, it's just a pile of rubble."

"I am trusting in God. He has a reason for sending me there. I can feel for Father Abraham when he received God's call to go. But I don't have wives and animals to provide for. I can get up off my sleeping mat and start walking."

James, teary-eyed but smiling, said, "Jesus trained you well, didn't he?"

"Yes, he taught us that we can make do without a lot of baggage."

Early the next morning, Philip was on the road again, going south toward Bethlehem, about five miles away. He was thrilled at the prospect of seeing the place where Jesus was born, which also was King David's hometown.

The sun had not yet come up as Philip passed through the village. He wondered where the birthing of his friend had taken place. The rolling hills south of the village were speckled with numerous herds of sheep

Aflame With The Spirit: Philip the Evangelist

with their shepherds. In his mind's eye he could see King David as a boy, enjoying the great outdoor life of a shepherd.

Leaving the Bethlehem hills behind, the road seemed to be following a dry watercourse between two ranges of hills. Philip started to feel the pull of a climb. About ten miles south of Bethlehem a road from the right beckoned Philip to turn onto it. But a voice said, "Stay on this road toward Hebron." Philip recognized the voice as that of the angel. "That I shall do. Thank you," he said aloud. Continuing toward Hebron with renewed vigor, meeting very few people, he was well aware of the guidance overshadowing him.

Hebron, another historical place. Near here, at the Oaks of Mamre, Abraham was told he was to father a son. I shall plan to spend the night at Hebron.

Using the training given him by Jesus to ask for a place to stay, Philip was taken in at the first home where he knocked on the door. The householder was as curious about Philip as Philip was about him and the city. Philip learned that even though Hebron appeared to be in a valley, it was reported to be the highest town in elevation in the whole of Judea.

The kind people with whom he stayed provided Philip with food for his journey. He was up and out at dawn the next day. He asked God's blessing on the home and friendly people who had been so hospitable to him.

He saw the gray clouds in the east beginning to show pink, signs of a glorious sunrise. *This is the best part of the day. I have always been fascinated with the beautiful, refreshing promise each morning offers those who love life and what it holds, despite these times of caution and uncertainty. Here I am, striking out on an unknown mission with nothing more to go on than complete faith and trust based on the word of an angel! I'm glad that I don't have to justify my actions to anyone but my friend Jesus. I wonder how far it is to Gaza.*

He had walked a couple of miles on the road descending from Hebron when he saw a good-size stream of running water curving in from the right and paralleling the road. It followed a shallow valley with low desert hills on each side.

The sound of an approaching carriage from behind caught his attention. Turning to see what it was, Philip was totally unprepared to interpret two sensations that reached his mind

Aflame With The Spirit: Philip the Evangelist

at the same time. The first was that which he was seeing. The second was a voice within his head. *My mind is playing tricks on me.* Then he recognized the voice of the angel saying, "This man is the reason you are here. He is an important person. Go and join him in his chariot." Philip accepted the statement. He was glad to know a real mission did exist for him here on this lonely, desert road.

Now, he was trying to make out that which was approaching, a beautiful white carriage with gilded decorations, drawn by a team of two magnificently matched, well-groomed, white horses. On the driver's bench, which was situated slightly above and behind the rumps of the horses, were seated two black men. Their movements were quick and their eyes alert. Seated in the carriage, which was mostly open except for a canopy, was a single person--a big, important-looking, bald, black man.

As the vehicle came closer, Philip could see he had very distinguished bearing and facial features. *Now that's truly a remarkable sight*, and mentally thanked the angel for giving him this rare opportunity. *But how am I going to 'go and join him' as the angel instructed?* Then he could hear the black man

Vada M Gipson

reading aloud. It was scripture! Was it from the prophet Isaiah? Yes! He recognized the passage: 'He was led as a sheep to slaughter, and as a lamb before the shearer is silent, he kept his mouth closed.'

The black man looked up from his reading and at Philip, and called to his driver to stop. A big, infectious grin showed strikingly white teeth. He said, "Good morning, sir."

Philip, smiling broadly, returned his greeting, "And good morning to you, sir. Your reading took me by surprise! Do you understand it?

"It's a riddle to me. I need someone to explain. If you can, come here and ride with me."

Philip climbed into the carriage and sat beside the black man. "I've never ridden in such style. What a beautiful carriage and team!"

The man signaled the driver to start the carriage rolling. "Thank you for the compliment. I have been to Jerusalem to worship, and am on my way home to Ethiopia. I work for the Candace."

Philip said, "I'm not familiar with the title. What or who is the Candace?"

Aflame With The Spirit: Philip the Evangelist

"She is the queen mother of the king. I am her Minister of Treasury, her trusted eunuch."

Philip nodded his understanding.

Tapping the scroll he was holding, the Ethiopian said, "I can never get used to how God is always showering me with His magnificent miracles. Here I am in the desert, of all places. In the desert, and He has sent me an interpreter!" He gave forth a jovial laugh that originated in the very depths of his being.

Looking at Philip, studying his features with those big, black eyes, Philip felt his love and sincere desire to learn.

He continued, "This is most remarkable. Since leaving Hebron this morning, I have--well, really, since I left Jerusalem, I have pondered this scripture." Then he asked, "Now, tell me--was the prophet talking about himself or someone else?"

Philip told him that he was writing about the Messiah. He went ahead and told the man about Jesus, and how, during Jesus' life, death and resurrection, he had fulfilled all the prophecies. Answering questions, he told him how, through the ages, God had been trying to reconcile humankind to God's self. Now, through baptism in the name of His Son, Jesus, it was possible.

The big man was absorbing every word. He looked beyond Philip into the desert hills. Philip doubted that it was the scenery at which he was looking. He appeared to be meditating on the powerful message Philip had given him. Then, looking at Philip, he asked, "Baptism, you say?"

Philip smiled and nodded, "Baptism."

Seeing the river alongside the road, the man gestured toward it and said, "Here is water. What is to stop me from being baptized?"

"Not a thing! It's a flowing stream."

"Whoa!" called the big, black man, and started to laugh in that deep, joyful, infectious way, and to Philip he said, "Let's go!"

He and Philip jumped out and disrobed down to their loincloths, leaving their outer garments in the carriage.

Both waded into the water. Philip took the man's hands into his and looked into those large, black eyes. He felt the power of the Holy Spirit begin to baptize them both. He asked, "Do you believe with all your heart, with all your strength, and with all your mind that Jesus is the Messiah?"

The big man looked heavenward and began to tremble, tears began to stream down the

Aflame With The Spirit: Philip the Evangelist

strong features of his face, and he answered, "I do, I do, I do!"

Philip didn't hesitate. He bent him over backwards until he was completely immersed into the flowing stream. The man was heavier than Philip could handle. With a big splash, he sat down on the river bottom. Philip helped him to his feet. He came up laughing his infectious chuckle.

Turning his face upward, in a loud voice, he said, "Thank you, God, for this sacred moment for which I've waited a lifetime-- a lifetime!" He brought his hands together, covered his face and began to sob.

Philip embraced him, and the Ethiopian then put his arms around Philip. There they stood, in the water, both soaking in the rapture of the moment. Philip said, "We will both long remember this event when the love of God is so--tangible, won't we?"

"The whole thing has been a miracle," he replied as the two released their embrace. "I feel so happy!" and began to laugh again.

Philip laughed with him. They waded out and dressed. At that moment Philip's mind went back to a scene when he was lying paralyzed in his family's courtyard. His prophetic daughters had just described this very day!

"And to have found you out here in the desert was a miracle!" He said once more. "In the desert! What a miracle." He turned his face heavenward, held out his big powerful arms in front of him, then high over his head. Bringing his hands together, then lowering them, holding them close to his heart. Still looking heavenward, he remained silent and great tears rolled down his radiant face. He said softly, "Great, and precious God of all that is, at last I have found You through Your wonderful messenger. I thank You for this great privilege, and I ask oh, Great One, to bless and protect him. Amen."

He turned to Philip, putting his hand on his shoulder, and said, "I have a very long way to travel alone. Your company would be welcome. What is your destination?"

"Thank you. I would enjoy the trip with you, I am sure, but my mission has been fulfilled with your baptism. This is as far as I am going. It will be your responsibility to spread the good news in your home country, that the Messiah has come," Philip replied.

Aflame With The Spirit: Philip the Evangelist

"That I will do, gladly. But I can't just leave you out here miles from population. Can we take you back to Hebron?"

"No, thank you. It's been my privilege to serve as a messenger to you and through you, to your people. But we'll part here. Go with God."

They embraced. "May God be with you, my friend," said the big man. "Shalom."

Philip responded, "Shalom to you."

The black man climbed into the carriage, and gave the signal to his drivers to move on. He settled back into the seat and picked up his scroll. He turned and looked back at Philip and waved.

But Philip was no longer there.

"Stop! Stop!" he yelled to his drivers. "Where is he?" Once more getting out of the chariot he walked back to where he had left Philip. The drivers came down from their seat and walked to the rear. They looked in the undercarriage, then in the water of the river. Nowhere could Philip be found.

The Ethiopian looked down the road, began to smile, then started to laugh. He said, "All right, men. Let's go. We've just witnessed another miracle." They climbed back upon their seats in the carriage and the trip to Ethiopia was resumed. The happy singing voice of the black man filled the vast amphitheater of the desert, deep and rich in tone. Now he had a commission to perform: an awesome, challenging responsibility to spread the good news in his home country that the Messiah has come.

And in all places for it to happen to him--a miracle--in the desert!

Chapter Twenty-one

As Philip started to raise his arm in farewell, he felt himself being lifted up bodily. Now he was standing on a strange road, his feet still wet in his sandals. The smell of the ocean was strong, but the scenery didn't match that around Caesarea. Where could he be?

To the north were buildings indicating a small village. He would go there, and ask what it is called. He hoped he wouldn't sound stupid, not knowing where he was. Approaching a shopkeeper, who had fresh produce in his stand on the main street, he asked, "Sir, what's the name of this town?"

"Azotus," answered the villager, "Where did you think you were?"

"I've just had a marvelous experience, and really didn't know where I was," Philip replied. He continued, "I'm a stranger to this part of the country. May I ask how far it is to Caesarea?"

"Um-m, I guess about sixty miles."

"To the north?" Philip queried.

"It must have been quite an experience. Yes, to the north."

"One more question, please. Where is the synagogue here in Azotus?"

"Just keep on this road. You'll see it near the center of town."

"Thank you. I have some good news to share with you and your neighbors at the synagogue. Why don't you come along?"

The shopkeeper hesitated and then said, "It's time for prayer anyway, and you've aroused my curiosity. I'll go with you." He dropped the curtain that had been tied to a post supporting a canopy over his stall.

Other merchants along the street were closing their stands, preparing to go to ninth hour prayer at the synagogue. Philip felt he was leading a parade, when he glanced back and saw how many were following him.

After prayer, the shopkeeper announced to the men assembled in the synagogue, "We have a visitor who says he has some good news for us." Looking at Philip, he asked, "Would you care to tell us your name?"

Aflame With The Spirit: Philip the Evangelist

Philip came to the front, stepped up on the dais, turned, and looking at the shopkeeper, said, "Thank you." Addressing the men assembled, he continued, "I am Philip of Julias, and I have wonderful news to share with you."

"Tell us," someone said.

"The Messiah that our people have been expecting for untold ages, has come!"

Someone said, "We've heard that before. What makes this one any different than the others?"

Philip replied, "I am his disciple, and can testify as a witness to his fulfillment of all the prophecies."

"Who is this messiah?" asked someone in the back of the room.

"His name is Jesus of Nazareth. He was born in Bethlehem because he is from King David's line. He went about the country teaching, preaching, and healing for about three years."

"Healing? What did he heal?"

"I was paralyzed from the waist down. I couldn't walk, I had to be carried everywhere. He healed me, and many, many others of all kinds of sicknesses."

"Tell us more about this man," a voice near the front prompted, and Philip told about His death and resurrection, and how everything Jesus had done fulfilled scripture.

Finally the shopkeeper said, "We must go back to our businesses. Will you come to my house for the night and talk to us more tomorrow?"

Philip said, "I'll be happy to. Thank you."

At the table, during the evening meal, the shopkeeper said, "I was in Jerusalem for Passover when Jesus was crucified. I thought there was something special about that man. Later, when we heard rumors his body had been stolen by you followers, I felt the priests were not being completely truthful."

Philip quietly watched his host and waited. He felt the man, who told him his name was Korah, had more to say.

"Then, this last Passover an innocent man was stoned to death--just for speaking!" He stared at Philip, then continued, "Again, I felt the priests in the Temple were being--what can I say--unfaithful to our religion?"

Philip reached over and squeezed Korah's hand. "Your feelings are correct. Some of the Pharisees are happy with the arrangement

Aflame With The Spirit: Philip the Evangelist

with Rome, and don't want anything to change it. So they are, not all of them, mind you, because some of them have become believers of The Way, as we call our movement, but some of the big, important chief priests are trying to stamp us out. The man who was stoned last Passover was a close friend of mine."

Looking sympathetically at Philip, Korah said, "I'm sorry." Then frowning again, he asked, "What about the Sadducees?"

Philip answered, "They do not believe in the resurrection for any of us, so, of course, they are not going to believe that Jesus rose from the dead. They have joined with the leaders of the Pharisees, and their lackeys, the scribes, to persecute us. It started during Jesus' ministry. They could see the people were following Him, and He was being accepted as the Messiah, but they wanted none of that. They might have to make some changes in their accommodations to Rome. So they killed Him!"

Korah stared at Philip for a long moment, as though he was struggling to understand. Finally he said, "It makes me sick. If you can't trust your priest, who can you trust?"

"God, and his Son, Jesus. They can be trusted."

The man gasped at the word, "Son," as if he had taken exception to the terminology, then nodded in agreement. He said, "I'm looking forward to hearing more tomorrow when you speak again at the synagogue."

Philip said, "Tomorrow's debate may end in many of you wanting to be baptized. We'll need what we call 'living water,' either a flowing stream or the ocean, and about knee deep. Do you have such a place nearby? A swimming hole or bath house?"

Korah thought for a moment and said, "The ocean is about four miles away. We could go there." Brightening, he added, "One of the farmers near town has built a dam across a ravine for water for his stock. He would probably let you use the lake behind it."

"Would water be running into it now?"

"Yes, I think so. It has a little creek, and we had a rain shower yesterday."

Philip said, "All right. We'll find out if it is still alive. If not, we will take a hike to the ocean."

The next day, after third, sixth, and ninth hour prayer times, Philip continued his teaching of Jesus' way of living, the kingdom

Aflame With The Spirit: Philip the Evangelist

of God, His Sonship, the happenings at Pentecost, the visitation of the angel, the conversion of the Ethiopian, and how he, Philip, came to be in Azotus.

The following day was the Sabbath. He knew better than to plan a baptismal event then, but the day after, the Lord's Day, would be perfect. The farmer had given permission to use his lake, and yes, water was still feeding it.

Korah and his family invited Philip to stay with them for as long as he wanted. From previous experience, he had learned that an overnight stay often turned into a week or more, so he was glad to accept their hospitality.

Such was the case at Azotus. Many accepted Jesus as the Messiah, repented of their transgressions, and were baptized on the Lord's Day. When he laid his hands on them, they received the baptism of the Holy Spirit, leaving the place rejoicing.

But many more heard Philip for the first time when he spoke at the synagogue on the Sabbath, and wanted to hear more. When he felt anxious to leave, to go on to Caesarea, he remembered he was doing his assigned duty.

He would stay until the Holy Spirit, or his angel, told him to move on.

The priest at the synagogue was among the last to accept Jesus as the Christ. He heard Philip preach from the first day, and stayed everyday thereafter to ask questions and be taught. He reminded Philip of himself and the apostles following the resurrection. Would they have believed if they had not seen Jesus themselves?

"Will you come to my home for a refreshment?" the priest asked Philip after he had been there two weeks.

"Thank you. I'll be happy to," Philip responded. As they walked the short distance Philip told him his father was the priest in his home village of Julias, and that he had been trained to take his place. The priest seemed to have more respect for him thereafter.

At the home, Philip was introduced to the priest's wife, a petite, dark- complexioned woman with twinkling blue eyes. She reminded Philip of his own wife, Hannah, who had died in childbirth. No longer did he experience twinges of guilt when he thought of her death.

Philip was surprised to see in the corner of the courtyard, lying on a pallet, a child. He

Aflame With The Spirit: Philip the Evangelist

was about four years old. Philip walked to the corner--yes, a canopy had been fixed overhead very much as he had over him in his father's courtyard when he was paralyzed. As Philip squatted down beside the boy, he felt a deep compassion for him and his parents. He asked, "Do you like having your own little corner of the courtyard, son?"

The lad stared at Philip, not answering.

Philip tried again, reaching for his hand, "Have you been paralyzed all your life?"

The child shook his head.

"Do you remember being able to run and play with the other children?"

A little smile brightened the boy's face, as he nodded, "Yes."

"Would you like to be able to do that again?" Philip heard a quick intake of breath from the boy's parents behind him. He seemed to read their thoughts: *Don't give us a false hope.* The only healings that had occurred since Philip's arrival were spontaneous ones following baptism. No one had asked.

The boy's smile broadened to encompass his whole face and he said, "Yes!"

"Can you sit up?"

He immediately sat upright.

"I have a special friend whose name I'm going to use, and I'm going to put my hand on the small of your back, like this, and I'm going to raise my other hand, like this, and I'm going to say, 'In the name of Jesus, heal this boy's legs and joints and give him the strength to rise and walk.' And then I'll tell you to stand before me, all by yourself. All right? Shall we do it?"

The boy's eyes were shining brightly as he nodded affirmatively.

Philip did as he had said he would, and when the boy was told to stand, he quickly rose to his feet standing on his pallet. His smile was reflected in Philip's countenance. Philip said, "Good boy," and rose to make way for the lad's parents to come near and embrace him. Laughter and tears were combined as the three hugged each other. Philip said, "Thank you, Jesus."

The priest broke away and came to Philip and embraced him. He said, "It had not crossed my mind that my son could be healed. I am ready to accept your Jesus, and be baptized with the next group."

"All right. I'll leave you to enjoy your family, but before I go I want to ask you something," Philip replied.

Aflame With The Spirit: Philip the Evangelist

"Ask whatever you wish."

"I must depart from Azotus soon, but I don't want to leave the congregation without a leader. Will you take the mantle?"

The priest looked at Philip very seriously. Then Philip saw a twinkle in his eye, and a smile twitching at the corners of his mouth. "It is an honor to be asked. Thank you. I'll be happy to. I may need some more training."

Philip breathed a sigh of relief. He had been hoping the priest would come around to accepting Jesus as the Messiah, but Philip had to wait for it to be his own decision. "Of course, we'll attend to that beginning tomorrow morning." As Philip left the home he said, "Don't let the little fellow get too tired for a few days."

Feeling that his mission in Azotus was in good hands, Philip left his friends a week later, and started north toward Caesarea. He traveled the main coastal trading route between Egypt and Jerusalem, so he was met and passed by many others. When he came to a division in the road, he took the one to his left, toward the water of the great sea. Korah had told him the city of Joppa, the only natural harbor in Judea, was at the end of that highway. The priest in Azotus had given him the name of a priest in Joppa, Benaiah.

Chapter Twenty-two

As Philip came nearer the ocean, the smell of the sea became stronger. He felt as though he were going home. He was walking across a fertile valley that extended northward as far as Mount Carmel, which he could see in the distance. He knew it was near Caesarea. Ahead of him now were gleaming white multi-story buildings behind a high wall. He thought the meaning fits the name Joppa, 'beautiful.'

It was nearly dusk when he approached a home to ask for lodging. A servant girl answered his knock. When he told her what he desired, she asked him to wait while she called her mistress. A few moments later, an unusually tall, gray-haired woman with warm brown eyes appeared at the doorway. She was dressed in a robe of soft purple linen.

When Philip told her his reason for stopping, she said, "Do come in. Sojourners are welcome in this house. Come in, come in." Turning to the girl, she said, "Prepare food for our traveler, and set a place at the table." To Philip, she said, "If you care to bathe before eating, water can be heated for the tub in the bathhouse."

"You honor me, madam. I'll accept your offer. I've come from Azotus today, and am in need of a bath."

"You are in need of a clean robe, then, too. I'll get one for you." Before Philip could protest, she flew up the stairs, and after a couple of minutes was back with a lovely maroon-colored linen robe. She handed it to Philip and said, "We'll clean the one you're wearing so you will have it when you leave."

Dumbfounded, Philip could only stammer, "Thank you."

Philip lingered in the tub marveling at the way the Holy Spirit was looking after his every need. He was curious about his hostess. She seemed to be the head of the house, making decisions as though she was accustomed to doing so; was able to discern need without words being uttered. And this home--a bathhouse of its very own! She must be rich to have such a place, and a serving girl, too.

Philip was in for another surprise. The dining table, instead of being just above ground level as he was accustomed to, with diners sitting on the floor, was on a pedestal, and he sat on a bench with four legs. The food served him was bread, cold roast lamb, fresh raw vegetables, and wine.

His hostess came to the table with him, saying, "We dine early. It will give me pleasure to see you enjoy your meal. Will you forgive me, if I don't join you in eating?"

Unused to such hospitality and courtesy, Philip made an effort to come up to her level and said, "Your presence will be my pleasure."

Philip prayed before starting to eat, and his hostess added, "So be it," to his prayer.

As he started to eat, she said, "We don't have many travelers stop here any more. Tell me about yourself."

Philip admired this lady. She certainly wasn't shy, and he was glad for that. If he told her about himself, then he could, perhaps, learn about her. So he told her who he was and how he came to be in Joppa. When he first used the name of Jesus, he distinctly sensed a reaction. He felt he would soon know what that meant.

When he had finished, he said, "Now, may I ask about you? You are a most unusual woman, and I am very curious."

She turned her head and looked at him from the corner of her eyes, as though she didn't quite believe him.

He continued, "It's true! I have stayed with many people, and never have I had the treatment you have given me."

"Thank you," she said, as she lowered her eyes. When Philip said no more, she breathed in and said, "About me?" Raising her head and looking Philip in the eye, she added, "I also am a follower of Jesus of Nazareth."

"You are?" Philip asked in surprise. "I don't remember seeing you in camp, and I'm certain I would have noticed you."

"I wasn't in camp. I became a follower the last time I went to Jerusalem and heard about Him, His crucifixion and resurrection. Someone was preaching about Him in the court of the Temple, and I was baptized, and became a follower."

"Are there others here in Joppa?" Philip asked.

"Yes, I have told many people about Jesus, but of course, I don't baptize. The priest at the

Aflame With The Spirit: Philip the Evangelist

synagogue is not happy with my activities, so our group meets on The Lord's Day."

"In the synagogue?" Philip asked.

"Yes. Why not?" She retorted. "It doesn't belong to him!"

Philip's admiration for this spirited lady went up another degree. In his mind's eye he saw himself as a priest with a woman--a woman!--such as this one starting a new sect within his congregation, and how he would feel about it. He smiled at the thought. He said, "Perhaps it would help if I talked to him. What do you think?" Asking an opinion of a woman brought him back to when he used to consult with Hannah, his wife.

"Would you do that? I would rather have him with us than against us."

"All right. I will do that tomorrow." He hesitated a moment before saying, "May I ask your name? I may need to know it tomorrow."

She chuckled and said, "I'm sorry that I didn't give it to you sooner. Everyone in Joppa knows it, so it didn't occur to me. I am Tabitha."

"Thank you."

Rising to her feet and picking up a lighted lamp from the table, she said, "Now, we've talked long enough, and you must be tired. I'll show you to your room."

Surprised to be offered a room, Philip caught his breath, and mumbled, "Thank you," as he also stood and followed her to the stairs leading to the upper floor.

Going through an open door and setting the lamp on a table, she said, "This is one of my sewing rooms, but--" She pulled a rolled sleeping pallet from a shelf and continued, "You can sleep here."

Philip saw a room, two walls of which were lined with shelves full of rolls of fabric. The wall opposite the door had two larger than average windows. In front of them was a table similar to the one downstairs where he had eaten supper. On the table was an assortment of colored threads and sewing paraphernalia. Pushed up to the table were benches, two of them. He was reminded of the Scriptorium at Qumran, where he had served as a scribe for a time, except he thought these seats would be more comfortable than those plaster benches. The fourth wall had shelves, too, next to the doorway, with neatly folded garments stacked on them. Philip wanted to ask about her need to have more than one

Aflame With The Spirit: Philip the Evangelist

room for sewing, but didn't because of the late hour.

His unasked question was answered when his hostess said, "Seamstresses will be here early tomorrow morning. You won't be able to oversleep."

Philip replied, "I am usually up with the dawn. I enjoy watching the sun rise while I pray."

"You are welcome to go to the garden in back of the house."

"You are very kind. Thank you so very much for your hospitality."

She replied, "I'm happy to have you as my guest. Good night."

"Good night."

The next morning, Philip followed directions and found the synagogue. It was the same priest whose name he had been given in Azotus, Benaiah. When Philip arrived, Benaiah was in a discussion with a class of older boys. Philip signaled that he would wait. Sitting cross-legged on the floor near enough to hear, he was reminded of the many classes he had taught in his home synagogue. Hearing Benaiah giving the same interpretation to scripture from the Torah that he had instructed, he wished he could enlighten the rabbi as well as the children with the new knowledge learned from Jesus. But, he wanted to talk to the teacher first. It would create an embarrassing situation if he were to break into class dialogue.

When the class was dismissed, Philip stood as the instructor came to him. He was about the same age as himself, Philip estimated. Peering intensely into Philip's eyes, he asked, "What can I do for you?"

"Are you Benaiah?" Philip asked.

"I am," was the brusque reply.

"I bring greetings to you from the priest in Azotus from where I have just come," Philip said.

Benaiah relaxed and smiled slightly. He said, "Thank you, and may I ask who you are?"

"I am Philip of Julias, a follower of Jesus of Nazareth. I am called an evangelist." He felt Benaiah's tension return. He continued, "Your friend's paralytic son was healed and he also became a follower of The Way of Jesus."

Benaiah gasped, but said nothing.

Philip continued, "May I share my experiences with you? I usually start preaching and teaching at the local synagogue,

Aflame With The Spirit: Philip the Evangelist

and would like you to hear my story first and be my friend."

Benaiah stared at Philip a long moment. Philip watched and silently prayed for the man. Finally Benaiah said, "I can't keep you from coming to the synagogue, but, frankly, I don't want to hear anything about Jesus of Nazareth."

"I'm sorry you feel that way--" Philip started to answer.

Benaiah broke in, "He's already caused too much trouble for my friends in Jerusalem."

Aha! Philip thought. *So that's the connection.* Aloud he said, "Jesus is the long-awaited Messiah. I have no doubt about that."

"You'll receive no help from me in pushing your sect."

Philip said, "I hope you will change your mind when you hear the good news I have to share."

"I'll debate you on every point," Benaiah answered, glaring at Philip. He continued, "My congregation is too cosmopolitan, aware of what's going on in the world, to be taken in by an itinerant preacher--or his disciple!"

"All right, Benaiah. We'll see which way your congregation goes." Turning to leave, Philip added, "Thank you for your time. I'll see you in the synagogue on the Sabbath." He hesitated, smiled, and added, "Shalom."

"Shalom," Benaiah mumbled.

Chapter Twenty-three

"May I stay a few days longer, Tabitha?" Philip asked his hostess when he returned from the synagogue.

"It will be my pleasure. How did your visit with Benaiah go?"

"I didn't make a friend of him, yet. He has prejudged Jesus from information given him by friends in Jerusalem--probably priests of the ruling council. He doesn't want to hear the truth. I told him that I'd see him in the synagogue this Sabbath."

"I'll tell my friends. We won't want to miss that!" Tabitha replied.

Philip spent much time alone in prayer until the Sabbath day arrived.

The day of the big debate was bathed in thick fog that occurs frequently in coastal areas. Tabitha's home was high enough to be above it, but the synagogue was not. Looking down on the billowy, soft-looking clouds, Philip thought, *It is symbolic--from above, the fog looks firm enough to walk on, but I know it is not. I must speak carefully today, and not depend upon myself--keep my mind on Jesus, and what he taught. He promised that the Holy Spirit would put the words in the mouths of us who preach his message.*

Philip and Tabitha walked to the synagogue together. Once there, Tabitha went to the women's section behind the partition in the rear of the assembly room. It was decorated with carvings that permitted the women to see and hear. Tabitha wanted a position in the front row so she wouldn't miss anything.

Philip also wanted to be near the front in the men's section. He found a few persons there already, and they were seated cross-legged on the floor. They stood in most synagogues. He nodded to them and sat down. The room filled quickly.

Benaiah, looking a little haggard, started the service. Some praise psalms were sung. Philip heard Benaiah's beautiful singing voice, and noticed that his spirit seemed to brighten, as did Philip's.

Aflame With The Spirit: Philip the Evangelist

After prayers, a scroll of scripture from the Torah was unrolled. From it Benaiah read how the people of Israel made themselves a golden calf to worship while waiting for Moses to return from the mountain with tablets containing the Ten Commandments.

Then Benaiah said, "We have with us today a visitor who is a disciple of Jesus of Nazareth. He believes this Jesus is our people's long-awaited Messiah. He would like to interpret the scripture for us today." He nodded to Philip, and moved to one side of the dais.

Philip returned the nod, stood, stepped up on the platform, and turned to face the room. He said, "Peace be with you."

"And also with you," was the response from the men.

"I am Philip, son of Jacob, priest of Julias. As Benaiah has told you, I am a believer that Jesus of Nazareth is the Messiah. Six weeks of preaching morning 'til night would not be long enough for me to tell you about Him and how He fulfills prophecy, but today I am going to relate the reading from the Torah to Jesus.

"This episode of the people building a golden calf creating something visible to worship is but one of many instances of falling away from God since humankind first left a one-to-one relationship with Him. God has been trying over the centuries to reconcile us, the creature He made in His own image, to Himself. But no! He gave us a will to decide for ourselves. We return to God briefly, but then go back to our old ways."

When Philip paused to take a breath, Benaiah chided, "You have made no interpretation."

Philip looked at Benaiah, smiled, and said, "Would you believe that the Christ was with God? He was in the cloud that led the people, in the manna that fed them, in the rod Moses used to strike the rock for water?"

"I can believe the Messiah was with God, but not your Jesus of Nazareth," Beniah retorted.

Philip responded to the remark with, "Our forefathers, who were following Moses, needed something visible to worship. Now, in our own generation, God has provided us with a vision of Himself, His own Son, Jesus!"

A noise resembling the sound of a snort was heard from Benaiah.

Philip continued, "He was born of woman, experienced the temptations of being human, and died a pain-filled death on the cross,

Aflame With The Spirit: Philip the Evangelist

taking the sins of mankind as a scapegoat, a new covenant with Jehovah, God's ultimate means of reconciliation to Himself."

Gasps from the men in the congregation told Philip they had not yet heard the good news of his return to life from the grave. He knew it would be difficult for them to understand how God could allow His own son to be crucified, the most disgraceful of all ways to die.

"I can site prophecy for everything that happened to Jesus during his life, ministry, death, and--" he hesitated briefly "--resurrection!"

"Don't try to tell us that story," Benaiah broke in. "We know you disciples stole his body, and passed that rumor that he rose from the dead."

Philip said, turning to address the man, "It's not a story, Benaiah. I am an eye witness!" Philip turned back to address the men in the congregation. Making appropriate gestures with his hands, he said, "I walked with him, talked with him, ate with him. He is alive, and the Roman soldiers have sworn he was dead when taken from the cross."

Benaiah walked to the center of the dais and asked the congregation, "Do you want

Vada M Gipson

to hear any more of this man's insults to our religion and beliefs?"

"No! No! No!" was the loud response.

Philip felt himself go limp. Stepping down from the platform amid jeers from the men in the congregation, he thought, *how else could I have handled this presentation?* At the door Tabitha and several other women joined him. After taking a few steps away from the synagogue, he was surprised to find three men had also joined them. His heart jumped as he thought, *have they come to harm me, as happened to Jesus in his home synagogue?* When one put his arm around him, placing his hand on his shoulder, all he felt was love and compassion.

Tugging at Philip to get him started walking again, the man said, "We must get you away from here. Benaiah may stir up those men to come after you."

Looking closely at the speaker, Philip saw his sincere concern for his safety. Starting to walk he said, "I've been staying at Tabitha's house. They won't go there, will they?"

"I'd feel better if you came home with me. She has no men to help protect you."

Tabitha spoke up, "Simon is right, Philip. I, too, feel you are in danger, and he and

Aflame With The Spirit: Philip the Evangelist

his sons can defend you better than we can. Simon is one of us. He can be trusted. Go with him, and God be with you."

Reluctantly, Philip said, "All right." Stopping and turning to Tabitha, he reached for her hand and said, "Thank you, dear lady, for your gracious hospitality. I shall never forget you. Keep the faith."

Tabitha, who had been looking into Philip's eyes, lowered her gaze, and bowed slightly to him. Withdrawing her hand, she said, "It has been my pleasure. I hope to see you again someday."

Turning to Simon, Philip said, "Lead on, my friend. I am in your care."

As Tabitha and the other ladies stood and watched them go, Simon, Philip, and Simon's two sons turned toward the business district of Joppa.

Philip guessed Simon to be about forty-five years old, and his sons, early twenty's. All three men were of burly build. He surmised that each one could defend himself physically, quite well.

As the four men walked briskly toward Simon's home, he said, "We're tanners. I hope that won't offend you."

Philip hesitated a moment, but controlled his outward expression and said, "Jesus has changed many of our ideas that we used to hold dear, hasn't he? He sees the real person. His honesty and sincerity are the important factors."

"Many Jews of the old religion still believe that we are contaminated and won't have anything to do with us."

Philip slowly replied, "That you must handle dead animals in your business is a matter of your own personal cleanliness." He hesitated momentarily and continued, "That's the way I think Jesus would look at it. He knows people must work, and making leather is an honorable profession."

"Good! You've just made me feel the best about myself since I became a follower of Jesus of Nazareth."

Philip was amazed at the words that came from his mouth, and thanked the Holy Spirit.

Simon continued, "I would like to hear more about Him. I feel there's so much that I don't know."

Philip chuckled and said, "He's my favorite topic. I'll be glad to tell you as much as I can."

Simon stopped at a courtyard door, turned to face Philip, and with a serious frown said,

Aflame With The Spirit: Philip the Evangelist

"As much as I would like for you to stay here for awhile, I fear for your life. Benaiah is not above rounding up a mob of thugs and coming after you. I think you should leave early tomorrow."

Philip felt uncomfortable, but could do no more than agree, "Thank you for your love and concern. I'll do as you say. But, meanwhile," he added with a smile, "we'll talk about Jesus."

Chapter Twenty-four

At dawn the next morning, Philip again found himself on the road, admiring God's handiwork. The next town was Lydda, about fifteen miles inland. Simon had given him the name of the priest there, Lael, but he didn't know his attitude toward Jesus. Because the road was the only access to and from Joppa, Philip had many traveling companions, even at this early hour. As he walked along, his thoughts were, *I wonder if there is safety in numbers. No! I can't allow myself those thoughts, I must depend on the Holy Spirit to protect me.* He asked himself, *Where did I go wrong yesterday with Benaiah? Perhaps I declared Jesus' Sonship of God too soon. I should have given them more of his teachings and events that fulfilled prophecy, and led the men gradually to realize for themselves that Jesus is the Son of God. On the other hand, Simon told me that Benaiah is a Pharisee, with strong ties to the priest families in Jerusalem. He would never accept Jesus as the Messiah no matter what I said! Well, I have a lifetime to fill with ministry to Jesus--He knew we would run into opposition and scoffers. These are the ones that keep us alert to possible errors. We must learn from our mistakes and keep true to our objective.*

Philip's attention was diverted by the sound behind him of a wagon being pulled by running horses. He stopped, turned to see it fast approaching. He jumped back because it seemed to be coming too close to where he was standing. The driver began stopping the team of horses right next to him. Four or five men jumped out of the wagon, and came to him.

One man said, "You're the man who spoke in the synagogue in Joppa yesterday?"

Philip looked sharply at the man. *Had he seen him in the congregation? He didn't recall that he did.* "Yes," Philip answered with his kindest voice. "I spoke yesterday. Why do you ask?"

"You claim a mortal man is the Son of God?"

"My claim is that Jesus, the Messiah, is immortal. He was God in human form. Do you think that a God who created heaven and earth cannot come to us in the body of a man?"

The man answered, "I'm not here to debate you. I'm here to give you what you deserve for insulting the religion of our fathers," and he struck Philip on the left jaw with his doubled-up fist.

Philip reeled sideways. The stoning of Philip's friend, Stephen, crossed his mind. *Are they going to kill me here?*

Just as he had almost regained his balance, he was struck again on the other jaw. A blow to his stomach doubled him over. An uppercut caught him under his chin as he came forward. Philip fainted and fell to the ground.

The men picked up stones and hurled them at Philip's body, striking his head repeatedly.

Philip found himself above the scene, watching the men pelt his body, but was free of it and felt no pain.

Within five minutes, the ruffians climbed back into the wagon, turned around, and left Philip for dead.

Immediately Philip was enveloped in an intense white light. He sensed peace and harmony and immeasurable love. The face of the Lord became visible in the light. Philip felt

Aflame With The Spirit: Philip the Evangelist

supreme happiness at seeing his Master again. He heard him say, "You must go back to the physical world once more, Philip."

Philip could not voice his protest, but sensed the Lord knew of his desire to remain with him.

"Your mission is not yet finished."

Philip looked at his beaten body lying at the edge of the road. People were walking on by it, barely giving it a glance.

Reading his thoughts, Jesus said, "Your body will heal."

Philip mentally argued that he was abandoned on the road, and no one knew him.

Jesus said, "Friends are coming for you now. You must go back."

Reluctantly, Philip agreed, as he gazed sadly once more into the kind eyes of his Lord. Instantly, he was again in his body and felt intense pain all over it. He wondered if he could move at all. He lost consciousness at the effort.

The sound of a horse-drawn wagon penetrated his hearing. *Oh, No!* He thought *they're coming back. Maybe they'll think I'm dead, if I lie still.*

The wagon stopped next to where he lay, and some men jumped down. One came to him and said, "Yes! This is Philip. He's had a real beating--I think he's dead. I don't see him breathing."

"I was afraid of that," another voice said.

Is it Simon, the tanner, from Joppa? Philip thought.

After some hesitation, Simon continued, "Well, we'll have to bury him. No one else will."

Philip tried to move, to utter a sound, but he was unable to even open his eyes.

One man turned him on his back from the doubled-up position on his right side in which he had been left. The pain caused him to black out again. He felt nothing as one sat him up, and placed his strong arms under Philip's armpits, while the other helped lift him into the wagon by taking hold of his legs above the ankles. Thinking he was dead, they took no care to lay him down carefully.

Consciousness returned to Philip as the wagon was rolling to a stop. He still could not move, even an eyelid. He heard Simon say, "We must stop and tell Tabitha."

"I'll wait here to keep those scoundrels from stealing the body."

Lying there Philip questioned himself as to what he could do to keep from being buried alive. Deep down, he believed he had seen the Lord, and had been told that his mission was not yet complete, but he hadn't expected the beating on the road, either.

Tabitha and the seamstresses came out of her house with Simon. They were all weeping as they viewed Philip's body lying in the wagon. Simon said, "Drive on to the tombs. We'll bury him, before anything else can happen to him." He walked with Tabitha and the other women behind the wagon.

Philip heard Tabitha ask, "How did you know Philip had been killed?"

Simon answered, "Some rough-looking men came to the house this morning, looking for him. He had left already, but I told them nothing."

Tabitha said, "They came to my house, too. I wouldn't let them in."

Simon replied, "I became worried about him on that road by himself. Something told me to go there. I'm glad I did!"

When Philip heard that, he knew his vision had been real. No matter how serious his situation looked, he would survive somehow to complete the mission he had yet to do, whatever it was.

He heard Simon say, "Here we are. I wonder where we can bury him?" The driver, whom Philip guessed was one of his sons, jumped down from the driver's seat and said, "We can put him right in this spot." He walked to the wagon for a tool used for digging.

Philip, feeling the presence of the Lord, uttered a weak moan.

"Did you hear that?" asked the young man. Everyone came to the wagon and looked at Philip.

"I heard him groan! He's not dead!" the young man continued.

"I heard it, too! Let's take him home quickly," Tabitha said.

As the driver again climbed into the seat to turn the wagon around, Simon said, "We'll take him to my place. We can protect him better than you can in your house full of women."

"Yes, Simon, that's what you said yesterday," Tabitha hastily replied.

"My mistake was allowing him to leave here alone. I should have sent one of my sons with the wagon to take him to Lydda. But while he is recovering, I think he'll be better off at my place."

Aflame With The Spirit: Philip the Evangelist

Philip moaned a little louder.

Both Simon and Tabitha looked at each other in silence. Tabitha finally said, "We must take him someplace and clean his wounds. I have the better facilities. You may leave one of your sons as a guard, if you wish."

Simon admitted, "You're right about having better facilities, and that's a good idea. I'll have Obed stay. You'll need him to help lift Philip."

"Thank you, Simon," Tabitha hesitated and then added, "Don't blame yourself for what happened to Philip. I probably would have let him start off by himself, too."

At Tabitha's, Obed gently stripped Philip of his clothing and carried him to the bath, where his cuts and wounds were carefully washed.

Philip was aware of everything, but he was still completely paralyzed except for an audible moan that escaped now and then.

After the bath, his body was gently patted dry, and healing ointment was put on the raw places. Obed carried him to the bed in Tabitha's sewing room.

Philip was glad to be free of their handling, in a nice clean bed, in a safe house. He had faith that his paralysis would be healed because of his vision experience. So, he now relaxed and drifted off to sleep.

He had no idea how long he slept, but when Philip awakened, he heard the voices of women in the room talking softly. Opening his eyes, he thanked God for that ability. He then turned his head in the direction of the voices, and again thanked God. Seeing the two seamstresses at work, he wondered, *Do I dare try my voice?*

"What day is this?" he asked, and the women jumped at the sound of him talking.

One woman quickly left the room to summon Tabitha. The other said, "This is the third day after the Sabbath."

Tabitha entered the room with the one who went to fetch her. She said, coming and kneeling by his bed, "Praise God, you're awake! How do you feel?"

"I'm sore all over, but I can talk and move. I was paralyzed when you brought me here."

"Do you know what happened to you?"

"Yes. Except for periods of unconsciousness, I was aware of everything."

Surprised, Tabitha asked, "Then you know that we nearly had you in a grave?"

Aflame With The Spirit: Philip the Evangelist

For the first time, Philip smiled and said, "Yes. I was desperate to let someone know that I wasn't dead yet."

Tabitha said to the woman beside her, "Go tell Obed the good news, will you please?" To Philip she asked, "Can we bring you something to eat?"

Philip, smiling, said, "You know the way to a man's heart, don't you. I'm starved. But I'd like to try going downstairs, rather than asking you to bring it up here."

Obed and the woman came into the room. He said, "Father will be so glad to hear that you finally woke up. How do you feel?"

"I'm feeling better all the time. I want to try my legs to go downstairs and eat something. I know you've carried me from place to place, but would you go ahead of me down the steps, so if I fall, you can catch me?"

"I'll be glad to."

The women left the room, and Obed helped Philip to his feet, and held his garments to dress him. Gradually they made their way down the stairs, one step at a time.

Meanwhile, Tabitha had sent her servant to Simon's to tell him the good news of Philip's recovery. She set food out for Philip, of which he ate but a small portion.

Soon Simon arrived. He said, "You gave us a big scare. We thought you had been killed."

"I know, Simon." Philip struggled to rise to his feet. "I want to embrace you for coming to my rescue, but if you return it, touch me lightly. I'm still sore in places." Philip placed his arms around Simon, who very carefully returned the embrace.

Philip released him and Simon stammered, "Blessed is the tanner who is embraced by a rabbi. I never thought I'd live so long."

Philip, in turn, his eyes filled with tears, said, "Most rabbis don't know the value of the human who just happens to be a tanner. I want you to know that I sincerely appreciate what you've done for me. Between you, Obed, and Tabitha, you've saved my life."

Philip sat down again, followed by the three. Simon said, "I had to come looking for you. I couldn't get on with my work, something made me get out the team and wagon and start after you."

Philip said, "You know who it was--the Holy Spirit. I don't know why I had to receive the beating, but I was protected from dying by your actions, guided by God's Holy Spirit."

Aflame With The Spirit: Philip the Evangelist

"Well, the next time you leave, you're going in our wagon, with my boys and me to guard your safety."

"All right. I think I'll accept this lady's hospitality for another day or two to recover some strength before I attempt the trip again, and I thank you, all of you."

Tabitha said, "Your recovery has been remarkable. I think the Holy Spirit has been in your room, doing some healing."

Obed said, "I was sure you had some broken bones, but they appear to be all right now."

Philip said, "Praise the Lord! He told me in a vision that my mission in life isn't finished."

Tabitha said, "Vision? Would you care to share it with us?"

Philip said, "Yes, I would, but right now, I think I'd better lie down and rest. Thank you for the food."

"Thank God, that I can serve you."

Chapter Twenty-five

Philip remained in Tabitha's home regaining his strength and recovering from the beating. It took more than the "day or two" that he had expected. In fact, he was still there when the next Sabbath came.

When Tabitha indicated that she would be going to the synagogue, but didn't expect Philip to go with her, he surprised her by saying, "I wouldn't miss it! I want to see Benaiah's face when he sees me walk in."

"Aren't you afraid he will have the men attack you?" she asked.

"I'm going to trust in the Lord. Simon and his sons also will be there. No, I'm not afraid."

So it was that Philip accompanied Tabitha to the synagogue, timing their arrival to be well after everyone else's. Tabitha went to the women's section, and worked her way to be near the divider.

Aflame With The Spirit: Philip the Evangelist

Philip spotted space for him to sit on the front row, directly below where Benaiah would stand. He then looked at Benaiah, who was seated at the left side of the dais. Philip watched him as he made his way to the place he planned to sit.

At first Benaiah paid no attention as to who it was making his way to the front. When he realized it was Philip, his body jumped as he grabbed the arms of the chair and involuntarily started to rise but caught himself and remained seated. His face turned ashen white. He returned Philip's stare, then averted his gaze, closing his eyes and leaning back in his chair. Philip wondered if he had fainted. The room became silent as Philip walked to the chosen spot and seated himself. Philip felt all the eyes in the room on him. Turning to look at the man on his right, he nodded a greeting. He then turned to nod to the man on his left. Neither was among the men who beat him.

Benaiah stood to start the service. He couldn't keep from looking at Philip, and Philip locked his eyes with him every time. Benaiah said, "Before we begin singing, I wish to acknowledge the presence of Philip, the disciple of Jesus of Nazareth, in our congregation."

Philip distinctly heard surprised reactions, and he thought *the murderers are among us.*

Addressing Philip, Benaiah said, "I thought you had gone away. I haven't seen you all week."

Philip responded, "When the time is appropriate, I would like to share my experiences of this week with these people, if I may."

Benaiah nodded, and announced the praise psalm to be sung. His singing voice was not too good, Philip noticed. He thought, *Benaiah is still recovering from the shock of seeing me alive and well. Thank God, my wounds are pretty well healed.*

Then came prayer and the reading of the Torah. It seemed to Philip that Benaiah was rushing the perusal of the scripture, as though he were anxious to be finished with this encounter with Philip. Benaiah gestured with his hand toward Philip to come forward. Philip thought, *He can't bring himself to give me a courteous introduction.*

Philip rose to his feet and stepped up on the dais. Benaiah watched him approach. Philip felt his eyes examining the visible

Aflame With The Spirit: Philip the Evangelist

wounds on his face. Then Benaiah stepped to the side of the platform. The room was silent. Every eye was on Philip.

He turned and stood silently looking at the faces of the men in the audience. Yes, near the back were his attackers, just across from where Simon and his two sons were seated.

He humbly said, "I praise God to be here this morning, able to talk to you and tell you of God's mighty works this week." With more energy, he said, "Look at the wounds on my face." He pushed the sleeve of his robe up to expose his forearm and continued, "These bruises on my arm. I have marks like this all over my body."

When he hesitated, someone asked, "What happened to you?"

Philip looked at the questioner, and repeated his question, "What happened to me, you ask? I was walking on the road to Lydda and was attacked by a band of thugs, who beat and stoned me and left me for dead. And do you know why?"

"Why?" someone asked.

Philip's voice was full of vigor as he shouted, "Because I believe Jesus of Nazareth is the Christ, the Son of God. For that I was killed!" He looked at the men, and everyone in the room was silent.

After a few seconds wait, Philip continued very dramatically, "Yes, I was killed, and my murderers left me alongside the road for the vultures to devour me. And do you know what happened to me then?" Not waiting for a reply and looking at Benaiah continued, "I went to heaven. I saw my Lord and Master Jesus, the Christ!"

Benaiah blanched at the remark, but held his tongue.

Changing his tone to one of merriment, Philip continued, "Oh, it was peaceful there. I wanted desperately to stay with Him."

Pacing across the platform, he turned his head and sternly looking at his audience said, "But the Lord told me that I must return to that poor beaten body, as He has work yet for me to do."

"Ha!" erupted out of Benaiah. "Do you believe this drivel? How much more do you want to hear?"

"What he has to say." "We want to hear it all." "Be quiet, Benaiah."

"Thank you, men. I have much more to tell you. That was only five or ten minutes on the

Aflame With The Spirit: Philip the Evangelist

first day of the week, and the whole week is full of the wondrous works of the Lord."

"Go ahead. Tell us all."

Philip continued with the drama of nearly being buried alive, and his miraculous recovery. He concluded with, "I've asked the Lord why He allowed me to receive the beating and stoning. The answer has been revealed to me that He needed to prove to you people, right here in Joppa, that He had the power to rise from the dead." Softly adding, "And I am living proof that He still has the power." Whispering now, continued, "I was dead." A little louder, "Nearly buried." Loudly, he said, "But now I live." Shouting, he said, "Praise be to God!"

Instantly applause broke out from the congregation. Philip, smiling, held up his hands, and waited for them to settle down. When it was quiet again, he said, "I would like to invite each one of you to accept Jesus as the Christ, the Son of God, and be baptized in His name for the remission of your sins. We can go to the beach for the water. I'll lead the way."

Philip stepped down from the dais, not even looking at Benaiah, and headed straight for the door of the synagogue. From the stirring behind him, he knew that many were getting ready to follow.

Most of the congregation was baptized that day. Philip remained in Joppa for six weeks teaching, preaching and healing. Benaiah and his henchman had not joined the saints, as the followers of Jesus called themselves, and he continued to test Philip.

When the time came for Philip to leave Joppa for Lydda, Simon and Tabitha accepted the responsibility of shepherding the new flock of believers. And Simon was true to his word: he and his sons drove him in the wagon.

Chapter Twenty-six

Sitting on the driver's seat with Obed was Philip, as the wagon made its way toward Lydda, a small town inland from Joppa, located by a river. They had been quietly riding along. Simon, the tanner, and the other son, Rinnah, were keeping a watch toward the rear, taking no chance of having a surprise attack on Philip again.

Obed quietly and thoughtfully said, "Philip, I've been thinking, and I need to know how my idea strikes you."

Philip knew that both Obed and Rinnah were believers. Feeling that he knew Obed quite well, because of the time they spent together, he was growing fond of him. Obed was almost like a young brother. He said, "Suppose you tell me what it is you've been thinking, and I will try to give you my opinion."

Obed hesitated before saying, "What would you say if I asked to stay with you in Lydda?"

Philip sensed Obed had something deeper on his mind than just having a holiday away from Joppa. He softly said, "Tell me what you mean, Obed."

As though he were weighing his words, Obed slowly said, "I think I've received a call to serve the Lord, as you are. I can travel with you, help you with things, and learn from you."

"So it wouldn't be just Lydda, but the next place, and the next?"

"Yes, that's what I've been thinking. Would you let me stay with you, if Father gives me permission?"

Philip put his arm around Obed, placing his hand on his shoulder, and said, "I would be pleased to have you with me, Obed. The Master had us go out in twos. I learned the wisdom of that when I was beaten and left for dead." Philip dropped his arm and brought his hand into his lap.

When Obed said nothing, just smiled, Philip continued, "I'll ask your father, if you would like."

Obed beamed his brightest smile, "Would you? That would be wonderful."

Aflame With The Spirit: Philip the Evangelist

Just then Simon happily asked, "And just what are you going to ask me?"

When Philip proposed that Obed remain with him and learn how to become an evangelist, Simon's demeanor became more serious. "It means I'd have to hire someone to take your place, Obed."

"Yes, I know, Father," he answered.

"I need to give it some thought."

Philip said to Obed, "I must tell you my desire is to go to Caesarea and remain there for the rest of my life. However, my greatest desire is to go where the Holy Spirit leads me, and if it's not Caesarea, so be it."

Obed answered, "Caesarea is only two days journey from Lydda. So, if you get there, that may be as far as you will go?"

"Yes. However, I'll do as I am led. If I'm needed someplace else, I'll go there."

"Um," was all Obed said.

"I was in Ceasarea several years ago on my training mission, and made some very good friends. I've been wanting to go back ever since."

Obed brightened, "If you get to Caesarea, and receive confirmation that you will remain there, I'll use it as a sign that I'm not meant to be an evangelist, and will go back home."

Philip smiled, "By that time you should know if you are to be an evangelist. I didn't know that's what I'd become when I started following Jesus." He couldn't visualize Obed as an evangelist, but neither did he expect Peter, the fisherman, to be able to stand up and speak as he did.

Simon, the tanner, took Philip to the home of a cousin in Lydda. He told Philip that they, too, were believers in Jesus of Nazareth. A big man answered the knock on the courtyard. He looked enough like Simon to be his brother. Philip was astonished at their similarity. They were welcomed and invited inside.

Simon introduced Philip to Dara, his cousin, and asked if Philip could stay with him. Simon explained that he was an evangelist for The Way, and had found an adversary in Benaiah in Joppa.

Dara said, "We'd be honored to have you stay with us. We have space only in the courtyard for you to sleep, but you're welcome."

Philip said, "Thank you. That's where I usually sleep."

Aflame With The Spirit: Philip the Evangelist

Simon said, "My son, Obed, wants to travel with Philip. Will you have room for him, too?"

Obed gasped, and looked at his father quickly and then at Philip. He said, "Oh! Thank you, Abba."

Dara, smiling, said, "Of course, we have room for Obed. Both of your boys have filled out a lot since we last visited. I think they're going to look like us, don't you, Simon?"

Dara's wife and three daughters had been observing from the cooking area of the courtyard. Dara said, "Rebekah, come see Simon and his two 'little' boys."

Rebekah and the girls came forward. She said, "Yes, they have surely grown--just like our 'little' girls."

Philip saw three comely young ladies, probably in their early teens. They plainly were interested in looking at the young men, and vice versa.

Simon said, "I have some food in the wagon for you. Rinnah, will you bring it in?"

One of the girls said, "I'll help," and all three left with him.

Dara laughingly said, "A lot of help they'll be!"

Rebekah asked if Simon could stay for the noon meal, which she was preparing. Simon said, "Thank you, we can visit while we eat, and then we have to start back to Joppa."

Philip and Obed went with Dara and his family to the synagogue on the following Sabbath. Dara introduced them to Lael, the priest, who ask Philip to speak. Philip gave the good news of Jesus of Nazareth being the Messiah. He could feel no animosity, and most of his listeners appeared to be interested in his message. He turned to Lael and asked, "May I meet here tomorrow with those who would like to know more?"

Lael, in turn, asked his congregation, "Do you want to meet with these men tomorrow?"

Many indicated that they did, so Lael, turning to Philip and said, "Tomorrow morning. We'll combine the boys classes with the men to hear your teaching."

Philip said, "There's one more thing I'd like to ask. Among Jesus' followers were women. He never excluded them, and always welcomed them. Could we also include those women who would like to learn more?"

Lael appeared to be a little uncomfortable with that request, but he again turned to the congregation of men and asked, "What about it, men? Will you come if women are invited?"

Silence at first. Then someone said, "My wife would be interested. Having women there won't keep me away."

Then another, "Me neither," and many others agreed.

Thus Philip began teaching and healing as he had been trained to do. The second day brought out more people, as did the third. Philip assigned the children to Obed, who was delighted to start his ministry. They met in a separate room of the synagogue.

Lael was attending, but it was too soon to assess his acceptance or rejection. Lael was impressed with the healings. All in all, progress was satisfactory with the new classes.

While at the home of Dara, Philip was enjoying the antics of the three daughters. He realized his own girls were approaching the ages of these. It was obvious they were drawn to Obed, who lapped up their attention. Philip wondered if his young ones had yet become aware of boys. He noticed that Dara and Rebekah took care that the girls and Obed were never left alone together.

One evening Dara asked Philip to go to the roof with him for a private conversation. Philip couldn't help but wonder what was on Dara's mind. It was dusk, but light enough to see clearly. When there, Dara sat down on the thatch and invited Philip to do the same.

Dara nervously said, "I understand that you are a single man, have I heard right?"

Philip looked sharply at Dara before he answered, "Yes. I have been married, but my wife died in childbirth six years ago, and I've never remarried."

"Did the child live?"

"Yes," Philip answered brightly. Thankful that she did he continued, "Praise the Lord." He hesitated momentarily and added, "I have four daughters living with their grandparents in Julias. Why do you ask?"

"First, tell me how old are your children?"

"My twins are ten, the next is eight, and the youngest one, six. Now, tell me why this need to know about my family."

"Well," Dara turned to look out over the rooftops and continued, "My oldest daughter is sixteen and isn't betrothed yet." Turning to look at Philip, he added, "I would like you to consider becoming my son-in-law."

Philip controlled an urge to laugh. *Marriage to one of his daughters was out of the question, but I'll have to be diplomatic about how I reject Dara's proposition.* Before saying a word, Dara added, "I have a goodly sum set aside for her dowry. She'd be a good wife. Rebekah has taught her how to cook and sew and all the things women do. She's a big help to my wife, and I wouldn't accept anything less than what she's worth."

Philip mentally went through all the objections to the success of a marriage, their age difference; the nearness of her age to his twins; he being an evangelist, not knowing where in the world he might be led; besides he just wasn't attracted to her, and he had no money to procure a wife. In his culture, some of his objections weren't acceptable. Attraction and age difference meant nothing to most parents when arranging the marriage of their offspring.

Philip realized that Dara had stopped talking and was waiting for him to say something. He reached out and placed his hand on Dara's shoulder and said, "Thank you, Dara, for the honor of being offered your daughter in marriage. I have no doubt she will make a good wife, for someone." He removed his hand, and continued, "But I'm not the right person."

"But, Philip--"

"Marriage is a sacred covenant between a man and a woman. Each must contribute to the success of the contract and to the happiness of each other. That requires the presence of both. My life is one of moving around, and marriage would be impractical. I'm sorry, Dara." He hurried on to say, "I feel privileged to have been asked."

Dara hesitating, said, "I'm sorry, too. I thought perhaps you would consider settling here in Lydda. The people like you. We could very easily build another floor on our house."

"My life is dedicated to the Lord, Jesus. I am at His beck and call. When He tells me to settle down, then I will stop traveling. Until then, I must go from village to village, or country to country for that matter. And sometimes I may face great danger. No, marriage at this time would really be quite burdensome."

Dara seemed to accept Philip's explanation.

"Are there no suitable husbands in Lydda?" Philip asked.

Aflame With The Spirit: Philip the Evangelist

"Oh, sure. There are some men here, but to tell you the truth, I haven't seen any that I would let my girl live with."

Philip could identify with his sentiments. He would be particular about who his daughters marry. Brightening, Philip said, "Why don't you talk to your cousin Simon about Rinnah? I noticed the girls were quite taken with both boys when they were here."

Dara thoughtfully answered, "Yes, I noticed that, too. In fact that was what started me thinking I should get her betrothed. I wonder--"

"Physical attraction doesn't always guarantee a happy marriage, but it did in mine. My father arranged for me to marry my dream girl."

"I'm sorry, Philip." Hesitatingly he continued, "Stirred up memories must be quite painful." He sat deep in thought for a few minutes. "I have learned to deeply love my Rebekah. I suppose it's by slowly maturing. I do appreciate what I have in life." He looked at Philip and smiled. "Our conversation has given me a greater insight into your dedicated life."

"It has its moments."

Chapter Twenty-seven

Philip and Obed were told the next morning when Obed commented on Dara's absence that he had taken off for Joppa. No reason was given, but Philip suspected the motive was matrimony of his eldest daughter. Upon Dara's return, the news was broken to the family in private, at a time when Philip and Obed were at the synagogue. Philip noticed the oldest daughter did not join in the repartee with Obed, and tried to discern her feelings. Was she happy or sad? She remained aloof and withdrawn.

In less than a week Simon and Rinnah came to Dara's. As Philip and Obed were returning from the synagogue, Obed said, "That's father's wagon in front of the house. I wonder what has happened to bring them to Lydda again so soon."

Opening the courtyard door, Obed hurried to his father and embraced him, and then his brother, saying, "I've missed you two. How are things in Joppa? Are things working out at the tannery?" Then he noticed the men were in their fine garments and asked, "Why are you all dressed up?"

Philip saw none of the women, only Dara, in the courtyard.

Simon said, "We have some very happy news for you, son. Rinnah is going to marry."

Obed looked at Rinnah with a broad smile, and then back at his father. "Who have you gotten to be my sister-in-law?"

"Dara's eldest daughter."

Philip watched Obed carefully. His smile froze and his eyes glazed, but he recovered instantly and reached to embrace his brother again. He said, "You're a lucky man. She'll make you a good wife."

Simon said, "We've brought the ring, and can have the wedding as we have plenty of room for them at our home in Joppa. She's dressing now."

A beautiful bride came down the stairs, followed by her sisters and mother. Philip wondered, *what happened to the fun-loving youngsters that were here yesterday?*

She shyly approached Rinnah, who was gazing at her shamelessly. He took her hand,

and slipped the ring on her finger. Everyone embraced the bride and groom. Dara served wine, and Rebekah asked the other two girls to help serve food.

Soon all of the bride's belongings were placed in the wagon, and she was lifted into it. Her sisters and mother were also lifted into the wagon. Simon drove. Rinnah, Obed, Dara, and Philip walked behind it as they left Dara's home for Joppa. Friends and neighbors, seeing a wedding procession, fell in as it went past their place.

Philip thought, *What am I doing here? Wedding parties can last a week, and I can't be away that long. I have responsibilities here in Lydda to those who don't go and will come to class.* To Dara he asked, "If I remain here in Lydda, may I stay at your home?"

Without hesitating, Dara said, "I wouldn't think of you going anyplace else. Don't you want to go to the party?"

"Oh, yes! But some of the people in my class may not go, and I would be leaving them without a leader. I should stay."

Overhearing, Obed said, "Then I will, too."

Philip said, "No, Obed. It's your only brother's wedding. You go and enjoy yourself.

Aflame With The Spirit: Philip the Evangelist

I'll be all right. Don't worry about me. Give my greetings to Tabitha and all my friends."

Philip stepped out of the procession, and returned to Dara's home.

The number attending class the next morning was reduced, but Philip was glad he'd made the decision to stay. After class one of the students, a man named Ithra, approached Philip and said, "I have a friend who is paralyzed. I've told him about the healings you've done in the name of Jesus. He can't believe me. Would you go to his place and heal him?"

Philip's face lit up as he answered, "I'd be glad to. I was paralyzed once, and I know the horrible frustration it causes. You'll need to tell me how to find him."

"Oh! I'll take you there."

Philip later wondered why he turned to the priest, Lael, and said, "If anyone comes looking for me, I'll be at--" Turning to Ithra, he asked, "What's your friend's name?"

"Aeneas."

"I'll be at Aeneas' house."

"All right, Philip."

Philip and Ithra left the synagogue to walk to Aeneas' home, which was located on the north edge of town. They were about halfway there when a running child behind them called, "Philip! Philip!"

The men stopped and waited for the lad.

"What is it, son?" Philip asked, smiling at the boy.

Breathlessly he said, "Some bad men--came looking for you--at the synagogue."

Philip felt his heart jump within his chest, and his pulse quicken.

"Where are they now?" Philip quietly asked.

"Lael sent them to Dara's house--and then he sent me to catch you and--warn you."

Dara's house was toward the south side of the village, but it wouldn't take long for them to find that Philip wasn't there.

Philip said to Ithra, "These men are here to kill me. I must leave the village at once. I can't take the time to visit Aeneas, I'm terribly sorry." To the messenger he said, "Thank you very much. Go back now and give my thanks to Lael. Ask him to tell Obed and Dara when they return."

After the boy left, Ithra said, "I know of a place down by the river where we can hide you until they've gone."

Philip said, "You do? Let's go. I don't care to get another beating from Benaiah's thugs."

Aflame With The Spirit: Philip the Evangelist

As they walked briskly toward the river, Philip continued, "Benaiah must have seen that I was not at the wedding celebration, and decided to strike when I was alone."

Ithra led Philip upstream about a mile, traveling through shrubbery and trees, to a shelter of reeds and brush made to look like a pile of debris left by a flood. He said, "You should be safe here."

Philip peered inside and asked, "What is this used for?"

Ithra answered, "When I was young, a group of us boys found a similar cave after a flood. We used it as our secret hiding place until it fell down. We decided that we'd build another one, only stronger, which we did. We use it to watch wildlife, and to snare animals for eating."

"It's an ideal place for that," Philip said.

"I'll bring you some food this evening and try to find out where the men are that are looking for you."

Philip embraced Ithra. "God bless you, my friend. Thank you."

It wasn't evening yet when Philip heard above the whispers of the flowing river, the sound of footsteps nearby. He thought, *One person isn't making all that noise—two, at least.* Edging into the darkest corner, he decided to remain quiet and let them go on past. But they came directly to his shelter.

"Philip, are you in there?" A voice asked.

Then Philip recognized Ithra, and directly behind him was Obed!

"Yes, I'm here," Philip moved out of the darkness. "Obed! What happened?"

Obed said, "I kept thinking of you in Lydda, alone, and couldn't get you off my mind. I had to come and see if you were all right."

"But you're missing the wedding party!"

"I had enough. Rinnah and his wife and the others are having a good time, and that's all I care about. I needed to return to Lydda, and I'm glad I did."

"So am I."

Ithra was putting down bags of food. He said, "This should keep you two alive for a few days."

Philip said, "I won't be able to repay you, Ithra. All I can do is ask the Lord to bless you."

"That's payment enough. You have brought us a new way of life, and I'm sorry your stay is being cut short."

Aflame With The Spirit: Philip the Evangelist

Philip said, "Yes, so am I. But I shall write James in Jerusalem. Maybe he'll send someone to finish my work for me, and I'll tell him about your paralyzed friend."

"That would be wonderful, Philip."

"How far is the next town, and what is it?"

"The next town is Antipatris, across the border in Samaria, and it is between fifteen and twenty miles."

When Ithra said, "Samaria," Philip felt renewed strength surging into his drained body. *I'm almost home.* "Antipatris? Named for Old Herod's father?"

"Yes. Old Herod built a new city on the site of an ancient town. I haven't been there, but have been told it's a beautiful place. You'll have to cross this river and another one to get there."

"That won't be a problem, will it? These rivers aren't very deep, are they?"

"They won't be more than waist deep anywhere this time of year."

Turning to Obed, Philip said, "Well, partner, are you ready for the next adventure in this life of being an evangelist? Let's plan on leaving at dawn tomorrow."

Chapter Twenty-eight

"I've not known any Samaritans. What are they like?" Obed asked Philip as they approached Antipatris about dusk.

"Just like us! Some of them have remained faithful to our Torah and are Samaritans only because they happened to have been born in Samaria."

"Then why has there been animosity between our races?"

"Because they claim Shechem to be the most holy city, and the Jews proclaim Jerusalem. Also, because of intermarriage between idol worshipers and those left behind at the time of Babylon's taking the Jews into captivity, our race was considered polluted."

"Have you any worries about staying with a Samaritan family?"

"I may have once, but not any more. Some of my best friends are those I made in Sebeste."

"Oh! Good. I was thinking we should try to find a Jewish sign on one of these houses."

"Jesus taught us to pass the peace to the householder. If it is returned, we should stay there. If not, we are to leave it and look elsewhere."

"Then should we try this house that we're coming to?" Obed asked.

"All right." With a smile, Philip said, "We'll see how well you're being guided."

Philip knocked on the courtyard door. A man answered, looking them over as Philip said, "Shalom. Peace be to you."

"And to you, also, shalom. What can I do for you?"

"We're looking for a place to spend the night. Would you, perhaps, have room in your courtyard for us?"

The man hesitated, and Philip felt as though he and Obed were really being inspected. The man, still looking at them, said in a louder voice, "Vashni, come here." Philip wondered if he were calling his dog on them, so was relieved when another man appeared over the shoulder of the first. "These men want to spend the night. What do you think?"

The first man stepped back and Vashni asked, "Strangers in these parts?"

"Yes. We're evangelists for Jesus, the Christ. We hope to establish a congregation of believers here in Antipatris."

"We've never heard of him. How long do you expect that to take?"

"It depends upon the reception of the people to what we have to share."

Vashni turned to the other man and said, "They look harmless. We can share what we have with them for one night. What do you think?"

Philip noticed the respect each had for the other's opinion.

The first man said, "I'm willing, if you are."

Vashni stepped back and bowed as he said, "Please enter."

Philip said, "Thank you," as he and Obed stepped into the courtyard.

"We were about to eat. Will you join us?" Vashni asked.

Philip said, "That would be nice. Thank you. May we wash and pray first?"

"Oh! Of course. Over there is a basin and some water. Help yourselves."

As the four men ate, they exchanged their names. The other man was Zabad. He said to Philip, "I'm curious about you. Obviously,

Aflame With The Spirit: Philip the Evangelist

you're an educated man. What are you doing out--what was it you said--being an evangelist? I don't even know what kind of a job that is."

That was the type of invitation Philip relished receiving. It gave him the opportunity to leisurely tell his story and that of Jesus of Nazareth, the way he liked to do it.

Many questions were asked to clarify certain points, and when Philip was finished it was nearly midnight. He and Obed were shown a room on the second floor in which they could sleep. Each was given a mat on which to lie.

After Zabad and Vashni had left them alone, Obed said, "We didn't get to know them. Do you think they are brothers?"

"I don't know. I wondered the same thing."

"Another thing, they seemed to be very interested in Jesus, but do you think they believe?"

"I don't know that, either. We'll have to wait 'til morning to see what they say."

"Do you suppose they expect us to leave tomorrow?"

"Obed! I can't read their minds any more than you can. We'll just have to trust in the guidance of the Holy Spirit."

"I'm sorry, Philip. I just feel a little anxious. This is the first time in my life I've ever slept in the home of a stranger. And I can't help but wonder about those two men."

"Trust in God. We're here for a purpose."

Philip's sleep was disturbed by someone entering the room, silently coming to where he lay, and lying down beside him. Instantly he was awake. He asked, "What do you want?" And that awakened Obed, who sat up immediately and looked Philip's way. The room was dark, lit only by starlight coming in a small window.

Obed asked, "What's the matter, Philip?"

Philip said, "One of the men is here beside me." He asked again, "What do you want?"

The man whispered, "I thought you would like me close to you, and hold you to me. Do you object to that?"

Obed jumped to his feet. Philip, still on the mat, but up on his elbows said, "Take care, Obed. I think I can handle this." To the man he softly said, "I can not allow you to hold me close in the manner you desire. Can we talk about it tomorrow morning?"

Just then the other man came to the door with a lighted lamp, and said, "Zabad, are you bothering our guests? Come, let's go back to your room, and let them get their rest."

Zabad slowly arose to his feet, and left with Vashni.

Obed said, "Whew! I've never had to fight in the dark before. I'm ready to get out of this place!"

"Yes," Philip replied. "We've been shown another kind of need, but physical violence is not the answer. As children, we were taught that when we strike anyone, it is an insult to God, as we are made in His image. We must never fight. That's what Jesus meant when He taught us to turn the other cheek when we are struck. He believed in alternate solutions to violence. So, we must do as instructed."

Chapter Twenty-nine

Philip and Obed arose at dawn, expecting to leave the house and look for another host with whom to lodge while they explored the possibilities of sharing their good news. To their surprise, Vashni was in the courtyard when they came down the stairs.

"Shalom," he greeted Philip and Obed. "I apologize for Zabad bothering you last night. I don't think he'll do it again."

Philip answered, "We thank you for your hospitality, but we thought we'd go elsewhere today."

"You're welcome to stay here for however long it takes to do your work. I would like to learn more, myself, of this Jesus of Nazareth," Vashni said.

Philip knew better than to look at Obed, who would be unhappy at staying another night. But Philip remembered Jesus' instructions not to move around--to stay at

Aflame With The Spirit: Philip the Evangelist

one place. So, he said, "If you're sure that we won't be a burden on you and Zabad, we'll accept your offer."

"It will be good to have your company. Now, I know you Jews pray at this time. Where would you like to do it?"

Philip asked, "Do you have a backyard?"

"Yes. This way." And Vashni led the men outside through the back door.

Vashni and Zabad were jewelry merchants. When they left the house, they gave Philip and Obed permission to come and go as they pleased.

Philip and Obed looked over the village that day, for signs of Jews or a synagogue. They found neither, but they did find a square in the center of town that seemed to be used for public speaking. The jewelry shop was just across the street from it. Philip said to Obed, "I wonder what kind of interest I can drum up if I get up on one of those stumps and start talking?"

"This I have to see!" Obed said teasingly.

"Oh, ho! You haven't heard an evangelist, until you've heard one on a stump in a square!" And Philip stepped up on one.

"People of Antipatris! I have good news to share with you! Come closer, so you can hear me well."

Men started to gather around Philip. Obed stood beside him, facing the group. Women stopped their shopping, but remained where they were to hear what Philip had to say.

"You know the prophecy of God sending a Messiah, his Anointed Son, to save humankind?"

No response from the crowd.

"You are acquainted with the Torah, aren't you?"

"Yes," was answered by several.

"Well, do you remember that God promised to send a savior from David's line to rescue us?"

"Yes!" Many answered this time.

"My good news is that He has come!"

"Where is He?" someone asked.

"He's sitting at the right hand of God, His Father, right now, and He has sent us a comforter, His Holy Spirit to be with us forever."

As Philip talked, the crowd kept growing larger and larger. When the sun was about to set, he said, "May I come back tomorrow and tell you more?"

Aflame With The Spirit: Philip the Evangelist

"Yes! Yes! We'll be here," responded the people.

"All right. I'll be here, too. Shalom."

"Shalom to you, good friend. Yes, we'll be here!"

As Philip and Obed started walking toward their temporary dwelling place, Vashni joined them. When Philip asked him the whereabouts of Zabad, he answered, "He always goes home ahead of me to prepare the evening meal."

"There are no servants or housekeepers in your household?" Philip asked.

"We manage to look after ourselves without any kind of help. We share in the housekeeping, and we must buy everything we eat and wear as we don't have time to raise a garden or take care of animals."

Obed asked, "Are you and Zabad brothers?"

"No, we're cousins. We've been the best of friends since we were children. It was natural for us to take care of each other when--well, I feel I can trust you two."

"You can," Philip said.

"Zabad's father was away from home much of the time when Zabad was little. When he was home, he was mean to Zabad, his only child. Zabad idolized his mother, and when her husband was gone, she and Zabad were on good terms. But when he was home, she joined him in belittling Zabad.

Philip said, "I can see where Zabad would have difficulty maturing. That would cause battle with anyone's emotions.

"Confused emotions--yes, Philip, that's the description. He's an excellent artist, designs and crafts beautiful quality jewelry. We have customers from Ceasarea and Jerusalem who tell Zabad what they want, and he always creates a piece that's more beautiful than the customer can imagine. But he has never outgrown the need for a loving father. He looks for this in almost every man he meets. That was what happened last night--just a little boy looking for his father to love him."

"And you?" Philip asked. "Did you have a similar problem?"

Vashni, startled, hastily looked at Philip. He saw only intense interest and compassion. He hesitated and then said, "Yes. Our fathers are brothers, and they traveled together. My mother stood up for me against him, though, when he was home, so I didn't get the treatment that Zabad did."

"Your fathers are yet alive, do I understand correctly?"

Aflame With The Spirit: Philip the Evangelist

"Yes. They're old now, and don't travel anymore. My mother is dead, but Zabad's is still living."

Philip said, "Your and Vashni's experiences show the need for a good male influence during the developing years of a child. What about grandparents? Did you have any to fill the gaps?"

"No, our father's parents were killed in one of the armed uprisings, and they were raised by foster parents. They didn't receive very good treatment, either."

Philip said, "I think I might be able to help you and Zabad. I was in training to be a priest, and this type of healing was one aspect of the priesthood that I enjoyed."

"Oh? That's very interesting. Do you really think you could? I have a great number of questions I'd like to talk over."

"Yes, I think I could help both of you," Philip said as Vashni stopped in front of his courtyard door and opened it for them. Philip asked, "Do your fathers live here in Antipatris?"

"No. They live in Caesarea."

Chapter Thirty

After the evening meal was eaten and the utensils cleared away, Vashni told Zabad of his sharing their life story with Philip and Obed, and possibly Philip could help them.

Zabad said, "Do we need help, Vashni? I think we're doing all right."

Philip hurriedly said, "Do you remember what I told you last night about Jesus?"

Vashni and Zabad both nodded.

Philip continued, "He also taught us disciples how to heal."

"But, Philip, we have no ailment. We don't need a healing," Zabad argued.

"I understand that you both have had poor relationships with your fathers. Am I right?"

"Yes, you are correct. But that happened when we were children. We're in our middle age now," Zabad said.

"You are yet unhappy with your fathers, and memories of your childhood, aren't you?"

Aflame With The Spirit: Philip the Evangelist

Looking at Vashni, Zabad slowly answered, "Yes." Pausing reflectively, he turned his gaze upon Philip. "I have no desire to explore those painful times. I would rather, by far, that they remain buried and undisturbed. We have had no contact with our fathers for twenty years. Too much damage has been done already. Let us alone, I say."

Philip, rising to the occasion, said, "The help I possibly could give would be from God, in Jesus' name through the power of the Holy Spirit. I would be used merely as a channel to help you understand your fathers and why they behaved toward you the way they did. With this, you could become free of the hold they have on you, and thereby the animosity you have for them. Would you be interested in that, Zabad?"

Zabad clamped his jaws together. Taking in a small amount of air and forcing it out through his nose, he said, "Well, now that you've managed to pry into something that's--" He stopped short, relaxed a bit, looked up with an earnest expression. "Yes! I've wondered all my life what I did to make him hate me so much."

Philip felt compassion for both Zabad and Vashni. He said, "Let us all stand in reverence, and follow my words closely as I pray." He stood. The other three joined him. Raising his arms, looking upward, closing his eyes, he said, "Dear Lord Jesus, you told us where two or more are gathered in your name to ask, and we'll receive. We four are here asking in your holy name for the healing of two dear and related friends who, each in his separate way, has negative thoughts of his childhood. Thank you, dear Lord Jesus. Amen."

Seating themselves again on floor mats, he said to both men, "Try to put yourselves into the bodies of your fathers when they were little boys, left without parents. Do you get a sense of being lost, not knowing what will happen to you? Now some friends or neighbors take you in. You may be two more mouths to feed among too many children already." Philip paused looking at both men who were sitting with eyes closed. Then he continued slowly, "Can you feel the fear of the unknown? The anger and frustration at being left alone? The helplessness of being small and not able to defend yourself?"

Zabad began weeping softly. Vashni turned his head to look at Zapad, reached to put an arm around his shoulder. He slowly said, "It never occurred to me to think of them, and what they went through."

Philip continued, "You children were not the cause of the treatment you received. Your fathers behaved toward you the way they were raised, which was the only training they received, to be mean and rough, and that may have been necessary to survive in those days, but was all they knew."

Zabad was sobbing now. Vashni, pulling Zabad closer to him, said, "Yes, I can see it clearly."

"Obed and I will be going to Ceasarea when we leave here. Would you like me to look up your fathers and talk to them?"

Vashni released his arm from Zapad and looked sharply at him. He continued to sit, as in a trance, the tears rolling down his face.

Philip said, "Zabad, your mother was probably afraid of your father. She was too weak to stand up to him. She, no doubt, loved you very much and suffered in her heart when she couldn't defend you. Whereas, your mother, Vashni, was of a stronger nature, and was able to stand up to your father."

"Yes, you're right," Vashni said. "My mother was a strong woman. She and I didn't get along after I was grown because she was domineering." He meditated on this new perspective a moment, then saying, "Thank you, Philip. I think you have started us thinking differently about all of this."

Zabad was still sitting with eyes closed, but had ceased weeping.

Vashni tenderly asked, "Are you going to be all right, Zabad?"

He opened his teary eyes and, staring straight ahead, said, "Never before tonight have I ever stopped thinking of myself, and how unfair life has been to me. What a selfish person I've been." Hesitating, he continued, "I would like to see my mother again, and let her know that I now understand." Looking at Philip, he asked, "Will you act as a go-between for me? When I left, everyone was very bitter."

Under his breath, Philip said, "Praise the Lord! Thank you, Jesus!" Aloud he said, "We'll see how our work progresses. If it goes well, and today indicated that it will, it may be a few weeks before we leave for Caesarea."

Obed said, "I can carry a letter any time."

Philip turned to look at Obed and said, "Yes! That's the way we can get in touch with her. We'll write a letter." Turning to Zabad, he said, "Shall we do it right now?"

"Yes, I fear too much time has passed already. Let's not delay."

Vashni stood and said, "I'll get some writing materials."

When he returned, he handed them to Philip. Philip asked Zabad, "Would you like me to compose the letter?"

Zabad quickly answered, "Would you, Philip?"

Philip asked, "May I include your father in the salutation? It may be an awkward situation if your mother were to receive a letter from you that excludes your father."

Zabad answered, "Yes, as long as I am attempting a reconciliation, it may as well be with both of them."

Philip said, "I agree with you. I certainly do, and I think it's wonderful." He started writing. He noticed that his hand seemed to be guided rhythmically by an inspiring source. When finished, Philip read it aloud for Zabad's approval.

"You have worded it very well. Thank you."

Then Philip asked Vashni if he also wanted a letter to his father. He answered, "By all means. I feel the love you told us about last night is filling this room. I could put my arms around my father right now, if he were here."

"Shall I invite him to come see you, or do you want to go to Caesarea?"

Vashni said, "Make it the same as the one from Zabad. Leave it up to him. If he is well enough to come, we'd be happy to welcome him. If he wants me to go to him, that I will do."

When Philip had completed Vashni's letter, he then wrote one of his own to Abraham introducing Obed, asking Abraham to help Obed find the men's parents, and to extend hospitality to Obed.

Philip said to the men, "This makes me very happy. Just by offering to be friends with them you two will be free of the anger you've held all these years. We don't realize how much control our emotions have over our bodies. I know-- how well I know--it's like a torment. I told you that I was paralyzed, and--when I was forgiven of my sins I was freed of my paralysis!" He went on to say, "You've done your part tonight by having me write these letters. Their reaction and response will be their part of whether you are truly reconciled, or not. I pray they will accept your offer, but if they decline, don't let it bother you. All right?"

Vashni and Zabad nodded agreement, smiling at each other.

Zabad said to Vashni, "I'll be all right tonight. You don't have to sleep in my room."

That brought a big smile on all the men's faces, and Philip said, "Thank you, Lord. Truly I feel your glorious presence here tonight."

Chapter Thirty-one

Obed left at dawn the next morning for Ceasarea. Philip went to the village square and continued his preaching about Jesus of Nazareth as the Christ.

The Sabbath was the following day. Philip had learned of a small synagogue supported by a colony of Jewish merchants and tradesmen in Antipatris. He invited Zabad and Vashni to go with him, but they declined saying they had a house of worship they attended, and asked if Philip would care to go with them. Philip was tempted, out of curiosity, but declined saying, "Tell your friends the good news I am sharing with the people in your village, will you?

Vashni said, "Indeed we will. We've experienced His power right here in our own home!"

Philip was welcomed into the congregation, and invited to speak. He

Aflame With The Spirit: Philip the Evangelist

told of his experiences in Caesarea a few years earlier, and the events that had taken place since regarding Jesus' crucifixion and resurrection and the coming of the Holy Spirit. When he thought he'd talked long enough, someone said, "Tell us more," and others called, "More! More!" So he told of his most recent trip, starting with the instructions of the angel, ending with his visit with Zabad and Vashni. Someone said, "How can we be disciples of Jesus?"

Philip was surprised that someone was ready so soon to accept Jesus as the Christ. "Confess with your mouth that Jesus is the Son of God, your personal savior, release all your sins to him and be baptized in His name."

"When can we be baptized?"

"I was planning on having a baptismal event a week from tomorrow, the Lord's Day, because of His resurrection on the first day of the week. When I crossed the river not far from town, I noticed a good place for it. Will you be ready?"

"I'll be ready."

"Praise the Lord. May I pray?" Lifting his arms high, looking upward, Philip said, "Thank you, dear glorious Lord, for this day and your multiple blessings on these, your people, in Antipatris. And now as we go our separate ways, may you bless us and keep us, make your face to shine upon us and give us peace until we meet again. Amen." Lowering his arms, and turning to face the congregation once more, Philip said, "I have been speaking daily in the town square. I invite you to come down and listen, if you are free to do so. I hope to have many of the people of Antipatris come out to be baptized, too."

Philip heard a muttering sound as though these Jewish men did not want to share the news with the Samaritans. He said, "Jesus, himself, went through Samaria and many became his followers. He has disciples in Caesarea and Sebeste. The Samaritans are people, just like we are. Many even worship in a manner very much as we do, using the same scripture and claiming Abraham as their forefather, just as we do. We are cousins to each other. God made both races, in His image."

More mumbling, with no one speaking loudly enough for Philip to hear. He said, "Come to the village center, if you can. Thank you for your courtesy," and he stepped down and walked back to the home of Vashni and Zabad.

A week after Obed had left for Caesarea, a carriage came into Antipatris. It stopped at Vashni and Zabad's place of business. Philip had just finished his preaching for the day, and was ready to start toward the house. He was surprised when Obed jumped down from the carriage. Obed saw Philip looking his way and waved to him to come over. Philip embraced him and welcomed him home. Obed softly said, "The fathers are in the carriage--and Zabad's mother, too."

Philip's face lit up with a radiance showing his happiness. He went to the carriage, salaamed, and said, "I am Philip, who wrote you. I'm so glad you came to Antipatris!" He saw two elderly, distinguished-looking men with white beards and brightly beaming brown eyes. The woman was tiny. Her head, well covered, but lines in her face told her age. She shyly kept her eyes down.

One of the men said, "Thank you for your letter, Philip. You'll never know what it means to us to know our sons want to see us."

"I think Vashni and Zabad have gone home. May I ride with you to their house?"

"Oh! Yes. Come aboard, and Obed, too. He is such a nice, young man. He's been very helpful to us on this trip."

Philip climbed into the carriage. Obed went to the driver's seat. Philip asked, "Which of you is Zabad's father?"

"I am," the other man spoke. "My name is Uel, and this is my wife, Abigail. We, too, wish to thank you for your letter. You've made us understand ourselves better than we ever have. We hope to make amends with Zabad."

"It won't be difficult. He'll be so pleased that you have come." Turning to the other man, Philip said, "I'm sorry that your wife is not here to take part in this event."

"Yes, so am I. My name is Tobiah. We're anxious to see our sons. What are they like?"

"Well, although they aren't as gray as you, they look enough like you two that you will think you're looking in a mirror, and you two look like identical twins!"

"Yes," Tobiah chuckled, "We've always had trouble with people telling us apart."

Obed stopped the carriage in front of the house where Vashni and Zabad lived. He came to the landing, and assisted Abigail and Uel in getting out. Philip jumped out the other side and helped Tobiah to the ground. Obed asked Philip, "Shall I knock?"

Philip said, "No, let's take them inside the courtyard for the greetings," and he opened the courtyard door. The men were in the cooking area preparing the evening meal. Philip called, "We'll need four more places at the table. I've brought company home for supper."

Both heads bobbed up from their work and saw Obed and the others entering the courtyard. Zabad dropped the utensils and exclaimed, "Mother! Father! You've come!" and rushed over to embrace them. After hugging his mother, then his father, he returned to his mother to just look at her. She was silently weeping as she gazed upward into the eyes of her son. He took her very gently in his arms and held her close. Soon Zabad was weeping, too. He put one arm around his father, and Uel's arms encircled him and Abigail. All three were sobbing and laughing at the same time.

Meanwhile, Vashni walked slowly to his father, salaamed, and said, "Welcome to our home." Tobiah returned the bow, and said, "Thank you for asking us. We were thrilled to receive Philip's letter. We've come to talk and get to know you two--and apologize for the treatment we gave you boys when you were growing up. Philip has a depth of understanding that truly is most remarkable, and when he explained it all, it was then that everything came together. Can we be friends?"

"Yes. I, too, wish to start over and be friends with you."

"Then let's begin with an embrace."

Vashni towered over his father by a head. He reached out and gathered him into his arms like Tobiah was the son, and Vashni the father.

Philip and Obed, grinning from ear to ear, went into the kitchen area and found additional food to put on the table for all of them to eat. Philip's heart was so full of joy, he felt like praising God. Before he knew it, he and Obed were singing as they finished preparing the meal. Everyone ate. Tasty as it was Philip had the impression that it wasn't noticed, let alone having any idea what they were eating.

Philip and Obed cleaned the eating and cooking area and went to their room, leaving the sons and parents visiting, making up for years of neglecting each other.

Aflame With The Spirit: Philip the Evangelist

Obed said, "Abraham and Leah sent greetings. They are happy you are near and that you hope to go on to Caesarea. They were very hospitable and treated me like their own son."

"They gave me the same feeling. I love that man like a father. I suppose that's the reason I've always wanted to return." After pausing a moment, he continued, "The missionary work is going well here in Antipatris. I'm planning a baptismal event at the river next Lord's Day. I attended the synagogue last Sabbath and thought I had made some disciples. But I haven't seen any of those people in the square this week, so I don't know. I'll go again this Sabbath and find out." He added wryly, "I hope they don't behave toward me as Benaiah did in Joppa!"

Obed said, "I've been trying my evangelism skills on Tobiah and Uel on the way here. I think they are about ready to accept Jesus as the Christ."

"How wonderful! I am so happy the way everything is working out. Wouldn't it be something special to baptize all of them at the same time, because I think Vashni and Zabad are ready."

"I also tried my hand at healing. Abigail is such a frail, little person, and she wasn't feeling well enough to come. After I used your method of calling on Jesus' name and asking for a healing, she recovered!"

Philip raised his face heavenward and laughed with great joy until tears streamed down his cheeks. "Oh, Obed! The glories of God--how wonderful. Oh, do I ever remember my first. And how did that make you feel?"

"Well, Philip," Obed began to choke up. "To tell you the truth--it scared me! I guess I was just testing the power, and when I realized it really works and the awesome responsibility, I panicked."

"You didn't let on, though, I hope?"

"No. Then I wanted to shout for joy and could hardly control my emotions. I did sing a praise psalm. She's still all right. I think she's tired, but she made the trip without any trouble."

"Obed, I'm proud of you. You're going to be an evangelist yet!"

"One time Abigail said that she would like grandchildren before she dies."

"Well!" Philip stared off into space, continuing, "Now that's an idea. Let's give it some prayerful thought."

Philip and Obed deliberately kept themselves busy the next few days and out of the house as much as possible, giving the sons and parents opportunity to become friends. They attended the synagogue on the Sabbath, but were not asked to speak. Philip did not press, as he knew they had heard him the week before.

On the Lord's Day they went to the village square. Philip preached an invitation to make a commitment to become disciples of Jesus, the Christ, and be baptized. He said, "Obed and I are going to the river. Anyone who wishes to come with us will be welcome," and off they went. Many of the daily listeners followed.

Some merchants around the town center closed their shops, as did Vashni and Zabad, who went home and helped their parents prepare to be baptized. The team was harnessed to pull the carriage, so Abigail wouldn't have to walk.

When Philip and Obed arrived at the river they removed their robes, waded into the stream to where the water was about knee deep, and invited everyone to form lines. Before immersing the person, they asked each one if he or she was a believer. In Philip's line were two couples from the synagogue. His heart sang when he recognized the men. Vashni and his father, Tobiah, were in Obed's line, and Zabad and his parents were in Philip's. His spirit soared when he saw them. He felt the angels in paradise were singing in happiness. Many who were immersed were also baptized with the Holy Spirit, and spoke in tongues. The day ended with the group chanting praise psalms and prayers before returning to their homes.

During the evening meal at Vashni and Zabad's, Philip initiated the new converts into taking part in holy communion. He broke the bread and each ate and drank the wine in remembrance of Jesus and his death on the cross. Each participant experienced the presence of the Holy Spirit. Philip felt he never had been part of a more holy moment.

Chapter Thirty-two

Philip made arrangements through Vashni and Zabad to use their place of worship as classrooms. He wanted to train leaders to start the small study groups that had proven so successful in Jerusalem and other places. Obed and Philip each taught twelve persons. Zabad was in Philip's class. Vashni had said that he would watch the shop.

Ten days later, when it was time to go home, Zabad approached Philip with, "I have something private I'd like to talk to you about."

Obed was to be with them. Philip said, "Is it something Obed can hear, so we can talk on the way to your house?"

"Oh, yes, I just don't want everyone in town to know what I'm going to ask you."

Philip chuckled, and with a twinkle in his bright, blue eyes, answered, "You have me curious. I'll hustle Obed."

Obed joined them, and they started walking home. Philip said, "Now, what is it, Zabad? You are getting along all right with your parents, aren't you?"

Zabad answered, "Oh, yes! I have approached them to move here so I can be with them. They're getting along in years, you know, and need someone younger to look after them."

Philip said, "Why, I think that's a very good idea, Zabad. What does Vashni think about it?"

"Oh, he's for it--and for his father coming, too."

"What was your parents' reaction? Is that what you wanted to talk to me about?"

"No," Zabad hesitated. "Well, it's connected. Oh, they're thinking about it. What I want to talk to you about is an idea my mother suggested to me."

When Zabad said no more, Philip prompted him, "And that is?"

"She wants grandchildren!" Zabad stopped walking and turned to look at Philip. "I'm in my forties, Philip! I'm too old to marry and start a family, don't you think?"

Aflame With The Spirit: Philip the Evangelist

It was Philip's turn to hesitate. Obed, who had been taking everything in said, "Marry a widow with children."

"Yes!" Philip fairly shouted. "That's the solution. We have two or three who were baptized with the group. Do you know them?"

Zabad turned and the three resumed walking. He answered slowly, "Yes, I suppose I do, by sight, but I really don't know them."

"Well, make it your business to get acquainted with them, and decide on which one to go for," Philip said.

"I don't even know how to go about it, Philip. Can you help me?"

"Obed and I can find how many children each one has, and things about them, like how old she is, and who was her husband, but we don't want them to get the idea we're looking for wives for us, do we, Obed?"

Obed said, "Not yet."

Philip looked sharply at Obed and observed that he was serious.

Zabad quickly answered, "Oh, I probably know all those things. After all, I've been in business here for twenty years. I know who was married to whom, and when their babies were born."

Philip asked, "Do you feel anything for one over the others?"

They walked a few paces in silence. Finally, Zabad said, "Deborah. Yes, Deborah. She has a dignity that I admire. She has two children, a boy about ten I'd guess, and a girl around eight years old, and--they're well-behaved." Zabad began speaking more rapidly, "She's had no one to help her, and she's worked to feed and house the family. She's the one!"

Philip asked, "How do you think you'll be as a father? These children will be trained to look after themselves, and may resent their mother sharing her time with a stranger."

"I'll have to be careful, won't I, that I don't repeat the same mistakes my father made. I'll try to be friends with the children and everything a good father should be." Zabad added, "Will you act as matchmaker, Philip?"

Philip answered, "I'll tell you this, ask your father. It's rightfully his responsibility. I'm sure he will be thrilled. If, for whatever reason he doesn't want to, then I'll be happy to."

With a big smile, he said, "Thank you, Philip. You've been a big help."

Aflame With The Spirit: Philip the Evangelist

When Vashni was told that Zabad's father was going to bargain for a wife for Zabad, he said, "I, too, have been thinking that I should marry." Turning to his father, he added, "Will you find a wife for me?" He then turned to Zabad and said, "Maybe we can have a double wedding," and laughed joyfully.

Tobiah asked, "Do you also want a widow with children?"

"It won't matter. I just want her to be a believer in the Lord Jesus, the Christ. Everything else can be adjusted to."

Thus two happy fathers went hunting for wives for their sons.

Deborah was pleased to accept the arrangement. However, she didn't care to leave her home to live in the house where Zabad and Vashni had been living. She owned her own place, and bargained that he come live there. Yes, if his parents decided to move to Antipatris, she'd be happy to have them.

So Zabad and Deborah became betrothed, and Zabad started becoming acquainted with his future wife and children. Abigail was filled with joy. Immediately, she began playing the grandmother role and loved every minute, as did the children.

The hunt for a wife for Vashni took a little longer. Among the converts was a single woman in her mid-30's, Baara, who had been orphaned and raised by friends of her parents. Because she had no dowry, matchmakers had by-passed her. When Baara was suggested to Vashni, he was pleased, as she was comely to look at. Baara's foster parents were happy to bargain with Tobiah and a match was made.

Vashni's remark, made in jest, about having a double wedding was brought about. Two homes hosted the wedding feasts, one at Vashni's and the other at Deborah's. Their place of business was closed for a week so the men could concentrate on enjoying their wedding parties.

Philip and Obed continued their classes. One evening, on their sleeping pallets, in the darkened room at Vashni's, after coming back from Zabad's, Obed said to Philip, "We seem to attract weddings. What is it about us?"

Philip answered, "It's life, Obed. Survival of the species is the highest priority regardless of life form. For humanity, marriage is what separates us from being like the animals. Having children is proof that part of us is going to live on after we're gone."

Obed was silent.

Aflame With The Spirit: Philip the Evangelist

Philip asked, "What's on your mind? Are you having second thoughts about being an evangelist?"

"Oh, I was just thinking about my brother and curious how he's getting along with his wife." He hesitated, and Philip waited. "It really should have been me, you know. I am the first born."

"No, I didn't know. Do you think your father arranged for your brother to marry because you had chosen to go with me?"

"Yes. He didn't deliberately try to hurt me. I know that."

When Obed said no more, Philip asked, "You cared for the girl, yourself, didn't you?"

Obed hesitated before answering softly, "Yes." He quickly added, "But she'll never know, and neither will my brother."

It was Philip's turn to hesitate. He felt sad for Obed. Finally he said, "Dara has two other daughters, both of whom are quite vivacious. Are you interested in marriage at all?"

"I've tried to put it out of my mind, but-- these weddings bring the desire back to me."

Philip said, "I have an idea. Let me think and pray before we talk about it any more. All right?"

"All right."

Chapter Thirty-three

Six weeks sped by. Leaders from Philip and Obed's classes were teaching small groups in private homes. The parents of Vashni and Zabad had moved from Caesarea to Antipatris, and the newlywed couples were making the necessary adjustments to having another person to consider. Seeming to be happiest of all was Grandmother Abigail and her grandchildren.

One dusty afternoon a rider came hurrying into town. He went to the jewelry merchants' place of business and asked the whereabouts of Philip. Aware of Philip's previous trouble with the priest in Joppa, Vashni asked the rider where he was from and why he needed Philip. He said, "I am from Caesarea. I bring a message from the son of Abraham, a friend of Philip's."

Aflame With The Spirit: Philip the Evangelist

Vashni told him how to find Philip at the place of worship. He jumped on his horse and heeled it to a run.

When there, he came running into the room, and called, "Philip?"

Philip stood and went toward the man. "I'm Philip. Shalom."

"Shalom. I bring a message to you from Elmadam, son of Abraham of Caesarea."

"Yes! What is it?"

"Abraham is sick unto death. Elmadam asks you to come quickly. Can you?"

Without hesitation, Philip answered, "Yes. I must tell Obed, my partner. Please wait here."

Philip went into Obed's classroom and signaled him to come, which he did. He quietly said, "I am being called to Caesarea to heal Abraham. This is a sign that I've been waiting for. Remember I told you that I had an idea?"

Obed was staring at Philip, but seemed to comprehend everything that Philip told him. He said, "Yes?"

"It was to leave Antipatris in your charge. That way you will be serving the Lord, but will be staying in one place so you can marry and have a family. How does that sound?"

Obed's reaction was clearly mixed. He smiled at first, then frowning, said, "But, don't you need me to go with you?"

"I have the feeling that I'll be staying in Caesarea. And I do need you--here with the congregation in Antipatris. Ask the leader of this place of worship to be your partner. Since he is one of us, he'll be a good helper. I'll ride double with the man who has come for me."

Obed sadly asked, "You'll come back, won't you? We will see one another again someday, won't we?"

"Antipatris is on the main road to Jerusalem. I may be here more often than you care for. Yes, I'll be back. And you can come to Caesarea to see me, too, you know." Philip added, "I'll write to your father, and tell him to find you a wife, if you want me to. How about one of Dara's girls?"

Obed blushed as he answered, "Thank you, Philip."

They embraced. Philip said, "Give my thanks and farewell to Vashni and Zabad. Oh! This morning I sent a letter to Jerusalem with Vashni and his father reporting my experiences to James. If there's a response, will you send it on to me at Abraham's?"

Aflame With The Spirit: Philip the Evangelist

"Of course. Give my greetings to Abraham and Elmadam. Shalom. Go with God."

Obed sadly watched as the rider, who was already on his horse, helped Philip mount behind him, and away they rode to Caesarea.

Goodbye, my friend. You're going to reach your goal. Go with God.

About the Author

Vada McRae Gipson, author of *The Quests* and numerous articles in national and local publications, began writing after retirement. She had met her husband, Lee Gipson, through their mutual hobby of amateur radio. He planned to write as an avocation in his retirement. To support his interest, she attended the organizational meetings with him of the Siskiyou Writers Club. The writing bug bit her. After taking a correspondence course from National Writers School, she began selling feature articles to magazines.

Vada remains active in her local church as organist and Lay Leader. She is a Certified Lay Speaker in the United Methodist Church, Shasta District, California-Nevada Conference.

Aflame With the Spirit: Philip, the Evangelist is the second of a trilogy of biblical fiction books based on incidents and characters in the Holy Bible and first century historical writers. *The Quests* is the first one.

The Acts of the Apostles is one of Vada's favorite books of the Bible. She has enlivened incidents taken from the Gospels and the book of Acts with creative writing that gives immediacy to a familiar story. Her prayer is for the stories of *The Quests* and *Aflame With the Spirit* to be a blessing to you, the reader.

Additional books may be ordered from http://www.vadasbooks.com, www.authorhouse.com, or by calling 1-888-280-7715.

The Quests is also available on audiocassette and CD. They and personalized, signed-by-the-author books may be ordered from www.vadasbooks.com.

Printed in the United States
47715LVS00001B/91-207